HOPE

for the ANXIOUS *and* DEPRESSED

HOPE

for the ANXIOUS *and* DEPRESSED

A Biblical and Practical Guide for Christians Walking Through the Darkness

HOPE A. BLANTON &
CHRISTINE B. GORDON

B&H PUBLISHING®
BRENTWOOD, TENNESSEE

Copyright © 2026 by Hope A. Blanton and Christine B. Gordon
All rights reserved.
Printed in the United States of America

979-8-3845-4110-3

Published by B&H Publishing Group
Brentwood, Tennessee

Authors are represented by Don Gates, literary agent @
The Gates Group, www.the-gates-group.com.

Dewey Decimal Classification: 616.85
Subject Heading: ANXIETY / DEPRESSION
(PSYCHOLOGY) / MENTAL HEALING

Unless otherwise noted, all Scripture references are taken from the Christian Standard Bible. Copyright © 2017 by Holman Bible Publishers. Used by permission. Christian Standard Bible®, and CSB® are federally registered trademarks of Holman Bible Publishers, all rights reserved.

Scripture references marked BSB are taken from the Berean Standard Bible printed 2016, 2020, 2022, 2025 by Bible Hub and Berean Bible.

Scripture references marked ESV are taken from the English Standard Version®, © 2001 by Crossway, a publishing ministry of Good News Publishers. ESV Text Edition: 2025.

Scripture references marked HCSB are taken from the Holman Christian Standard Bible, copyright © 1999, 2000, 2002, 2003, 2009 by Holman Bible Publishers, Nashville, Tennessee. All rights reserved.

Scripture references marked NASB are taken from the New American Standard Bible®, copyright © 1960, 1971, 1977, 1995, 2020 by The Lockman Foundation. All rights reserved.

Scripture references marked NIV are taken from the New International Version®, NIV® Copyright ©1973, 1978, 1984, 2011 by Biblica, Inc.® Used by permission. All rights reserved worldwide.

Scripture references marked NLT are taken from the New Living Translation, copyright © 1996, 2004, 2015 by Tyndale House Foundation. Used by permission of Tyndale House Publishers, Inc., Carol Stream, Illinois 60188. All rights reserved.

Cover design by Matt Lehman. Author photo by Jen Hinrichs.

1 2 3 4 5 • 29 28 27 26

Christine: For Michael, who looked square in the face of my depression so many times and, instead of moving away, pushed in.

Hope: For Ray and our children, Cana, Thea, and Nias. For my parents, March and Sheila.

Acknowledgments

Thank you to Caroline Cobb, who encouraged us repeatedly to write this book.

And to Ashley Gorman, who makes everything better.

Thank you to Jen, Renae, Elizabeth, Rebecca, and countless friends for believing in this project.

And to the Lord, who has been near and kind to both of us in hard places for so many years.

Contents

INTRODUCTION

What Is Happening to Me?

The pain you're feeling is real.

The daily suffering you feel isn't something you made up. For a believer in Jesus, talking about how desperate you feel sometimes can be difficult. You know you're saved. You are seen and known and loved by God. You have the Holy Spirit, the Counselor. And yet, your life is still full of pain. Even though you belong to Jesus, the pain often takes the form of anxiety and depression.

We (the authors of this book) know this pain firsthand.

So let us begin by letting you into our stories—you know, the story behind the credentials we bring to the table. Yes, one of us, Christine, is a practical theologian with a theological degree (MATS) who often serves as an adjunct professor at a seminary. Yes, the other of us, Hope, is a (Christian) licensed clinical social worker who serves as a counselor in her local life. Yes, both of us founded At His Feet Studies, offering approachable Bible studies for women in every season because of our common love for God and his Word. But before all those milestones were woven into our stories—and sometimes even still to this day—the pains of anxiety and depression were woven deeply into our stories as well.

It is worth offering you a heads-up at this point that a few details we're about to share feel dark—and if you're not ready for that, perhaps come back to this when you are. But rest assured, the light is coming. The whole point of this book, in fact, is to offer you light and clarity in your darkness so you can understand what you're dealing with when you face anxiety and depression and, more than that, experience the stronghold of the God who cares about you and walks *with* you in the hardest of seasons.

So a bit of our stories.

I (Christine) was eleven years old and standing at the end of my driveway the first time I told God I wanted to die. At that point, I wasn't quite sure if God was real, but I wanted to put in a request just in case. It seemed like classmates and family members moved through their days with an excitement I just couldn't find.

What was the point of all the effort in life if it felt this hard? This sad? For years, I thought I had some flaw that no one else had, that no one else would understand. I had no language for "depression," so the weight I carried around I carried alone.

In college, the heaviness came and went. But in graduate school it barreled back into my life at full speed. Classes, relationships, even showers took more energy than normal. I was ready to end it.

* * *

It was hard for me (Hope) to explain what I felt at first. It came on so suddenly. I had been a worrier my whole life but had not really used the word *anxious*. But this was miserable.

When the panic attacks first started, they would show up even when my stress level wasn't that high. Days after, I would feel like a million fire alarms were going off in my head. My body couldn't do anything to calm down. It became hard to eat. Sleep was interrupted every night with deep fear and night sweats. I couldn't do much of anything except feel heightened and overwhelmed. There was no pattern in the type of event that brought it on. But once that ball was rolling, it was racing downhill fast.

The first time it happened, I had no idea what was going on. I was in my early twenties and had been a believer for about four years. It was foreign. Overwhelming. Confusing. Disorienting.

As I started to get help, I realized, Oh my, this is a thing. This anxiety thing is happening to me. And I soon learned through the stories of others that I was not alone. It was happening to others, too.

A lot of life has happened since we first experienced those debilitating symptoms. I (Christine) followed my questions about the pain in life, which ultimately led me to Christ. I came to know him in college. My questions about suffering landed me at Covenant Seminary in St. Louis where I parsed Hebrew verbs and translated Greek sentences in search of God's answer to my and others' pain. I sought to care for those struggling with loss while working as a chaplain resident in an emergency room and surgical ICU, as an intake coordinator for a large counseling practice, and as a Bible teacher to women in my local church and others around the country. I have attempted to explain not only God's response to pain in the world but many other parts of his Word as I've written Bible studies for At His Feet Studies with Hope for about twelve years now. Along the way I've struggled, sometimes greatly—other times hardly at all—with depression. My current doctoral studies have allowed me to dive deeper and more slowly into God's Word but always with an eye toward God's tender compassion for those who suffer.

As long as I can remember, I (Hope) have wanted to help those who were suffering and struggling with mental health. It wasn't until I became a Christian that this became a clear path for me. It was actually through my anxiety that I came to Christ. I started by working in alternative schools with at-risk youth in Philadelphia providing case management, counseling, and countless hours of listening to all kinds of stories of suffering and pain. I continued my social work education by earning a master's in social work. I completed three thousand clinically supervised counseling hours to become a licensed clinical social worker in the state of Texas, where I've been co-running a private practice for almost a decade. Along the way I've been on staff at a church caring for women, planning and speaking at retreats, leading Bible studies and trainings, and meeting with women in their brightest and darkest hours.

When Hope and I (Christine) met in Lincoln, Nebraska, in 2013, it didn't take long for us to figure out we were going to be friends. But we had no idea that God might use our friendship and partnership. God used Hope's experience, compassion, and clinical knowledge to love me extremely well in some dark days of struggle. I (Hope) was so helped by Christine's biblical and theological understanding of the fall and its effect on humans—particularly in the area of mental health. That was a game changer for me when I was really struggling. Over the years, we've seen Jesus use the hope that we've shared with each other to encourage others with that same hope.

What to Expect

In this book we will guide you systematically through definitions of anxiety and depression from biblical and clinical perspectives. We know how confusing it can be to try to make sense of your anxiety and depression in light of your Christian worldview. We promise to take your pain seriously because we've lived it. Using the biblical storyline of creation, fall, redemption, and glorification, we will help you understand how those intersect with your mental health. We hope to give you a resource that will clarify the conversation about depression and anxiety and offer tools to bring you some relief. Ultimately, we hope to point you to the hope that is only found in Christ, the Great Physician and Good Shepherd who provides many means to attend to your suffering.

Our Prayer for You, Dear Reader

We pray this book will encourage you saints who suffer.

We pray the tools we offer will relieve some of your suffering.

We pray it might offer categories for understanding how you got here, what you can do to push back against the effects of the fall, and where you're ultimately going.

And most of all, we pray you'll feel closer and more connected to Jesus after reading this book.

Chapter 1

Confusion and Misunderstanding

"Now may the God of peace sanctify you completely . . . your whole spirit and soul and body."

1 Thessalonians 5:23 ESV

Depressed? Try Harder

Becky felt exhausted as she looked at the pile of laundry, thinking it was an impossible task. *It's been a long two years, but I still feel heavy about it as if it was yesterday,* she thought to herself, as she closed her eyes and leaned back on the couch. The death of her mother hit her in ways she had never imagined it could.

For the past few months, Becky had struggled to enjoy much of anything. Sometimes she couldn't get out of bed in the morning. Other times she suddenly started crying and wasn't sure why. Often, she felt a deep sadness that was unfamiliar to her.

Becky tried never to miss church. She'd been active in Bible study for years, figuring out how to attend regularly—even though she worked part-time as a teacher's aide at her daughter's school. In a vulnerable text with her best friend, Becky mentioned how she was struggling. "I am not feeling like myself. I can't get through the sadness."

Her friend suggested talking about it with their Bible study leader, Sheila. Sheila was a kind older woman in the faith. So Becky had coffee with her later that week. Though it felt good to talk about her pain with someone who cared, Sheila seemed unsure how to help. She suggested Becky meet with her pastor.

Three weeks later, Becky finally made it to her pastor's office. She felt awkward sharing how she was feeling but was desperate for help. She told him all the details she could think of—even the ones she felt embarrassed about. The pastor's questions centered around Becky's prayer life and Bible reading. He sounded concerned but reassured her that everyone goes through sad times when a parent dies. He suggested that spending more time in the Psalms might be all the help she needed.

Becky left feeling ashamed and confused. *I have been spending time doing my Bible study lesson every week and trying to pray. What is wrong with me?,* she thought. She now felt embarrassed for wasting her Bible study leader's and pastor's time. She concluded that she just hadn't had enough faith. If she could just have more faith, this sad feeling would go away.

Becky resolved to try harder.

Stigma and Misunderstanding

Marc had been struggling with anxiety and depression for years. At first, he didn't know what to call it. Straight out of college he got his dream job of working as a high school choir teacher. He felt like he was really making a difference in the lives of his students through music.

After about five years, he started to notice symptoms of depression slowly creeping in. He began to care less and less about daily life, and he was more easily angered by things that used to not bother him at all. Then a deep sense of hopelessness became so heavy that all he could do was drink it away at night after his kids went to bed. On top of all of this, he started to have panic attacks at work that made him feel terrified.

Marc finally opened up to his wife about all he was feeling. She admitted that she almost didn't recognize him anymore and encouraged him to see a doctor. Marc was desperate, wanting relief, and he agreed to see someone. The doctor recommended an antidepressant and mentioned that he often saw men come in with similar symptoms.

Marc was hesitant at first. *I'm a Christian, he thought. Isn't this a crutch? Shouldn't I just be relying more on prayer?* He was reluctant but took the meds. After a few weeks, he began to feel better than he had in years. He fell in love with being a choir director again, felt less irritable at work, and enjoyed his children more at home.

When Marc's church posted a position for a new director of music ministries, he felt a surprising excitement. His wife encouraged him to apply. He loved being a member of his church and was hopeful to use his spiritual gifts to serve. Marc made it to the final interview, where the elders and the pastor asked him a series of questions about spiritual health. Marc felt he needed to share about his experience with depression and anxiety in the last few years, mentioning that he had been taking medication to help.

Marc was pleased with the interview. In fact, he was almost positive that he had gotten the job. When his pastor called him later that week and explained they would be filling the job with someone more spiritually mature, Marc was heartbroken.

When Marc asked him to elaborate, the pastor explained that the elders didn't feel comfortable hiring someone who was relying on medication for their well-being. With all the pressure sometimes placed on worship pastors, the elders were wary of hiring someone who wasn't "mentally stable."

It's Only a Spiritual Problem

Kristin didn't ever remember being anxious until she went to college. When she had her first panic attack her junior year, she wasn't even sure what to call it. None of her friends had ever mentioned anything similar, and she was hesitant to say anything about it.

Over the next semester, she only had one more panic attack. She assumed it was just a phase and that as she matured in the faith and dedicated more hours to serving others in her college ministry, those attacks—whatever they were—would not come back.

Thirteen years later, Kristin was thirty-three and had just given birth to her second child. She was having a panic episode almost every time she went to the grocery store. She was finding it harder and harder to drive herself places without her husband or a friend in the car. One Sunday, she had an episode at church during the message. She felt a tightness in her chest and began to have trouble breathing. With her three-month-old baby strapped to her chest, she slipped into the bathroom to try to figure out what was going on.

Embarrassed and overwhelmed, Kristin ran into Helen, an older woman she vaguely knew from Bible study. Between shaky breaths and tears, Kristin tried to communicate what was happening. Helen's face quickly grew concerned.

Helen put her hand on Kristin's shoulder and said, "My kids were hard when they were little, too. Have you given up your quiet time since you had the baby? Sometimes in that season I didn't put God first enough, and I felt anxious a lot." Kristin tried to take a deep breath as Helen concluded, "You know, all issues are spiritual issues."

Maybe Helen was right, Kristin thought. *These episodes got better in college when I spent more time with God.*

At a playdate later that week, a friend asked Kristin if she was okay. Kristin shared what was going on, and the friend suggested she should meet with a counselor because talking to someone can help. Her friend was quick to warn her that she really needed a biblical counselor because others could lead her astray.

A Downward Spiral

Michael had not been feeling himself. Long hours, frustrating meetings, and disappointing growth at the church he pastored had made preaching and caring for his congregation feel overwhelming. The most recent disappointment was an outreach event that went nothing like he had hoped, resulting instead in the local neighbors wanting the church removed from the school where they had been meeting. It was the last straw. He realized he was more alone, tired, and discouraged than he had been in years. Why should he even keep trying? What was the point of all his hard work? What, even, was the point of his calling? Or his life?

Michael became more and more convinced of his failings. He got in his car and started driving, aching to find escape from the sadness that seemed to wrap itself around him tighter and tighter. An hour later, he found himself at the front door of a friend, a pastor at another church with whom he'd often prayed.

After hearing his story through Michael's tears, the friend finally spoke: "Let's get you something to eat." The friend pulled his family's leftovers from the fridge, heated them up, and set them before Michael, who realized he hadn't eaten anything all day. "Come downstairs," the friend said. "You need to rest." Michael silently obeyed, feeling the heaviness in his limbs as he walked into the darkness of the basement's spare bedroom. He covered himself in a quilt, closed his eyes, and slept. Several hours later, his friend woke him, fed him dinner, and sent him home, encouraging him to talk to his wife about how he was feeling.

What About You?

Do you see yourself in any of these stories? Have you found yourself struggling with similar things and not known how to engage with them as a Christian? Often, when it comes to mental health and our theology about it, we feel intimidated, confused, and unsure of how to proceed.

You don't have to be a counselor or struggling yourself to have heard and been around conversations about mental health. According to a mental health poll conducted in 2024 by the American Psychiatric Association, 43 percent of adults say they feel more anxious than they did the previous year.[1] Depression is one of the most common mental health disorders in America, with twenty-one million struggling.[2]

And it's not just the adults who are struggling. According to NIMH, 20 percent of teens ages twelve to seventeen will experience at least one major depressive episode in their adolescent years.[3] Unfortunately, all professionals tracking this data are seeing a steady and continual climb in all categories, rising several percentage points for both anxiety and depression in recent years. The saints in the church are not exempt from this.

Depression and anxiety are not just things that happen "out there" in the world; they happen to believers inside the body of Christ. While faith can have a positive effect on these mental health struggles, it does not shield people from them altogether. And while we don't have clear data about the rates of these mental health issues in the church, we can expect those numbers to be comparable to the statistics listed above.

One Side of the Conversation: It's Only Spiritual

If you've ever struggled with anxiety or depression and opened up to others, you may have had all kinds of unhelpful and confusing things said to you. Perhaps you shared during a small group discussion how you felt, only to be given the advice of being more disciplined in your memorization of the Bible. Maybe you talked with a pastor who confirmed that it was a spiritual issue and cautioned you to be wary of counseling.

Many Christians aren't sure how to respond when someone admits they are having difficulty getting out of bed every morning or frequently experiencing intrusive anxious thoughts. They want to help but have never been given categories for why a Christian would experience this kind of suffering. It might be foreign to them, so they don't even know what they don't know. Your mention of "anxiety" may explain a very different experience for you than it has for them. In an effort to quiet their own insecurities about tackling the subject of mental health, many well-meaning Christians have shut down hurting brothers and sisters with quickly given trite advice, or worse, offered a dismissive statement that sometimes sends a struggler into the shadows of shame, afraid to come back into the light about what they are experiencing.

Some Christians believe every problem we encounter is a spiritual issue. Some believe all experiences of anxiety and depression are due to lack of faith. The reality of a fallen body in a fallen world isn't even brought into the conversation, nor are the sciences of biology, neurochemistry, and gastroenterology, which often study the various expressions of physical and mental fallenness. The dynamics of trauma, family origin, and social relations are not considered either. Factors that are "not spiritual" are dismissed, not considered contributors to the problem.

This way of looking at the world assumes our struggles with relationships, addictions, the church, and even God himself are only to be understood as a direct result of our personal rebellion and sin. And so we are told we need only to acknowledge this reality and turn away from our rebellion. Other people think anxiety and depression are an attack from Satan and that demons are causing their behavior. As for medication, instead of being considered a help from God, it may be understood as a crutch, something we lean on instead of him. If we take it, we're giving up and not using our faith to defeat anxiety or depression. Those who do use medications such as antidepressants are seen as spiritually immature.

These simple understandings and approaches leave only one pathway for change: Repent of your sin and increase your faith through prayer and spiritual disciplines. If we simply have more faith, believe the gospel more deeply, stop sinning, or defeat Satan's schemes, we won't feel anxious or depressed. If we spend enough time praying about our problems, God will take away the deep sadness we are feeling. If we just meditate on the right Scriptures, we will no longer have to suffer with these types of issues. If we call out to God in faith chants or sensationalized declarations, we will defeat the enemy, and our problems will evaporate for the rest of our lives. Like the assumption of Job's misguided friend Zophar, this approach assumes that another person's misery is only and always due to "sin that is in your hand" or "evil [that dwells] in your tent," and if you simply put those away, "you will forget your suffering" and "your life will be brighter than noonday" (Job 11:14 NIV, 15–17 CSB).

Now, for the believer—and as we'll explore more in the coming pages—sometimes the negative experiences of life *are* the result of our personal rebellion and sin against God. There's no denying that fact. But is *every* negative experience in the heart and mind of a believer due to this?

Sometimes past trauma, family upbringing, and social relations *can* be a way to avoid personal responsibility in the present. But is it fair to say these things have *nothing* to do with a struggler's anxiety and depression?

And the Scriptures *are* helpful in our battles against anxiety and depression (not to mention any other type of battle in this life!). But are there other sources of God-given help in this world that we are allowed to use in seasons of struggle?

In this book, we attempt to answer these questions with no, no, and yes.

For believers who have only heard this side of the conversation around anxiety and depression, they are often left wondering, *Am I allowed to take medication? Is more faith finally going to change things? Are there other tools or treatments I can use?* This confusion can leave you stuck.

(As a quick aside, we'd like to make clear that this position does not reflect every Bible-believing church, nor does it reflect the perspective of many biblical counselors—a biblical counselor being something we'll explore in chapter 6. However, this profile represents one side of a spectrum that people can sometimes hear in various Christian environments from fellow believers.)

The Other Side of the Conversation: It's Not Spiritual at All

While some of our Christian brothers and sisters have decided that all personal struggles should be treated like spiritual problems, others go to the opposite extreme and believe that the Bible has no insight to offer in the realm of mental health and have ignored it as a tool in this area. As medical and clinical practices have changed and improved over hundreds of years, some have mistakenly decided that spirituality and sin have nothing to do with our personal struggles with mental illness.

Anxiety and depression, specifically, have been relegated to the world of psychology. In this line of thinking, depressive and anxious thoughts are all a result of one's childhood home or solely brain chemistry. Mental illness is exactly that—illness. This can lead Christians to believe that humans hold no moral responsibility for their own mental state. Satan is not involved in our struggles with anxiety and depression and shouldn't be factored in. We should only think about anxiety and depression from a clinical perspective.

Where do all these different ideas about mental health leave us as Christians? It may seem like we have only two, mutually exclusive options: Either we can treat our anxiety and depression struggles by exclusively using spiritual remedies including repentance, prayer, pastoral counseling, and spiritual disciplines, or we can go outside the church and find resolution to mental health issues by using medication, psychiatrists, and specific counseling modalities such as EMDR (Eye Movement Desensitization and Reprocessing), IFS (Internal Family Systems), or others. This leaves us between a rock and a hard place, hoping there is a third option.

All this misinterpretation, misunderstanding, and confusion about mental health has led to Christians not only failing to receive the help they need but also experiencing shame for their struggle. In their fear of being labeled as spiritually immature or stuck in sin, discouraged saints keep their struggles hidden. They withdraw from their brothers and sisters, believing that while the gospel seems to "work" for those around them, they, for some reason, continue to fail. They doubt their salvation, their understanding of grace, and God's ability to heal them. Some, in their hope to improve their situation only through spiritual treatment, may refuse other God-given kinds of treatment until it's too late.

Too many struggling Christians have been left without a helpful framework to deal with mental health issues. Too many loved sons and daughters of God have limped through long seasons, believing there was no help for them in their pain. God, in his compassion, has provided many avenues of healing for those struggling with anxiety and depression. He has not left his people to suffer in shame and isolation. But to make use of the many tools for restoration that are available, we must first understand the extent of the damage that has been done by the fall, which happened in the garden of Eden—something we'll explore in the next two chapters.

Where Do We Go from Here?

How should Christians think about mental health? What should shape our understanding of anxiety and depression? Does being faithful to the Bible mean we see mental health solely as a spiritual issue? Does thinking about psychological struggles as medical issues exclude the need for faith? These are the questions we have struggled with over the years and will consider throughout this book.

Many Christians land in one of two unhelpful places when it comes to thinking about mental health. Both places have too small a view of God, sin, and redemption. As souls residing inside of a body, we must form a theology around mental health that includes the full counsel of God's wisdom.

On the one hand, and by way of recap from the information above, some believe *mental health is only tied to our spiritual lives* and therefore must only be treated spiritually. Personal sin is the core issue or biggest contributor to the problem. Therefore, healing only calls for repentance and faith. On the other hand, some Christians believe *all mental health issues are physiological* at their core. They must be treated medically and have little or nothing to do with faith.

Neither of these views give us the full biblical picture of anxiety and depression. The most pressing truth from the Bible is this: *There is good news for those who suffer!*

The redemption of God is as wide and tall and deep as the world itself. As far as the curse is found, so far does the healing extend in the kingdom of God. The Creator of our bodies created every natural law, moral order, and truth in the universe. He can employ a wide range of techniques, modalities, and processes for our healing and our good.

Though complete healing will not be realized until the fullness of the kingdom comes when Jesus returns, a measure of healing is possible now. You who are weighed down with the heaviness of depression or burdened with the relentlessness of anxiety, be encouraged. Your God sees you and will give his compassion to you through avenues you may not anticipate.

As we go on this journey together, we will be using several terms. In order to be clear about their meanings, we will define them here:

> **mental health:** A state of mental well-being that enables people to cope with the stresses of life, realize their abilities, learn well and work well, and contribute to their community.[4] While people differ in what they consider vital for solid mental health, most would agree that mental health is important for humans to function and engage in their lives.

> **anxiety:** A persistent feeling of worry or dread, which can interfere with daily life. It is not the same as occasionally worrying about things or experiencing anxiety due to stressful life events.[5] In a later chapter on anxiety, we will explore various anxiety disorders and what they look like in daily life.

depression: A mood disorder that causes a persistent feeling of sadness and loss of interest.[6] Like anxiety, depression has a major impact on an individual's daily functioning. In a future chapter, we will explore depression in depth and the different ways depression can show up in one's life.

clinical psychology (including counseling and social work): The study of human behavior, mental processes, and emotional difficulties. Counselors—whether they are a licensed professional counselor (LPC), a licensed clinical social worker (LCSW), or a psychologist—are clinically trained and use their training to make clinical assessments and offer help.

counseling: Assistance and guidance in resolving personal, social, and psychological problems; often done by a trained professional. "Lay counseling" is performed between fellow Christians who may have received some training but not a mental health degree.

theology: The study of God or God's view of a certain issue. A "theology of ________" is a study of what God says in his Word about that certain subject, so, for example, "a theology of anxiety" would be a view of how God thinks about anxiety.

DSM: *Diagnostic and Statistical Manual of Mental Disorders* is a handbook used by mental health professionals that gives descriptions, symptoms, and criteria to help them identify and diagnose mental disorders.

Throughout this book, we will answer the question, How should we as Christians think about mental health? As you deepen your theological and clinical understanding of these topics, you will leave with a framework that will help you know how to engage in a struggle with anxiety or depression, if you ever experience it, or engage with a loved one who struggles.

God's Holistic Care

Remember Michael, the pastor who was cared for by his friend? If the story sounded familiar, it's because you've probably read it before. Michael's story is a modern version of the story of Elijah in 1 Kings 19.

After the magnificent display of God's power before the prophets of Baal, Elijah learned that Jezebel was still after him. He felt all alone in his ministry of the true God and ran in his discouragement into the wilderness, sat under a broom tree, and asked to die. It wasn't a fellow pastor but the angel of the Lord who met him there.

Notice what the angel did. Though it was obvious that Elijah needed spiritual nourishment, correction, and encouragement, those were not the only avenues of the angel's healing. In fact, what Elijah needed first was food, which the angel cooked for him. Next came sleep, something the exhausted prophet desperately needed.

After Elijah's nap, the angel fed him again, giving him nourishment for the upcoming journey to Horeb, the mountain of God. God treated Elijah's depressive symptoms and despair holistically, beginning with his physical needs for food and sleep, followed by his need for spiritual encouragement and God's Word.

God's care for his people continues in both compassion and specificity. He will use all kinds of means to encourage, strengthen, and heal those who are afflicted. Take courage. And ask God to come near as you seek help for your suffering.

Questions for Reflection

1. Which story from the vignettes given could you most relate to and why?

2. Of all the ways that mental health has been handled in the church, which one have you seen the most? Why do you think that is?

3. Which views of mental health have you typically leaned toward the most?

4. What did you learn about anxiety and depression?

Chapter 2

Fearfully and Wonderfully Made

"For you formed my inward parts;
you knitted me together in my mother's womb.
I praise you, for I am fearfully and wonderfully made."

Psalm 139:13–14 ESV

It Wasn't Always This Way

Looking around at this world, a lot would make you think there never was a time when we were whole, healthy, happy people without shame or guilt. Sin and regret, death and decay are the waters we swim in. For those with long-standing mental afflictions, waking up every day with some sort of dread or despondency is all we've ever known. But it wasn't always this way. In fact, it was never meant to be like this—a beautiful world, twisted and distorted. We need to go back before we can go forward. We need to put on a pair of pre-fall, pre-sin, biblical glasses in order that we might understand how we got to where we are.

"In the beginning God created the heavens and the earth" (Gen. 1:1). So much beauty is contained in that one simple sentence—multiple days of creation, time, creatures, and life. God started with nothing and ended with a universe that is bursting with variety, color, and symmetry. On the first day, light was created, with its wavelengths and photons, spectrum, and energy. It filled the dark spaces and was separated from the night. The second day brought the sky, with its feathery clouds, pale blues, and a canvas for sunsets. The third day brought sunflowers and pear trees, roses and lavender bushes. On the fourth day, the sun was fashioned with its far-reaching warmth and energy for growth. The moon appeared and worked together with earth's gravity to make the oceans rise and fall.

The fifth day was a burst of sound and color, welcoming crocodiles and cockatoos, llamas and lemurs, painted dogs and tiny hummingbirds. But on the sixth day. . . . On the sixth day came the big reveal. God assembled the pinnacle of his creation, the height of his artistry. "Let us make man in our image, according to our likeness" (Gen. 1:26). God saved his best work for the sixth day, when he made people who look like himself. Who we are as humans hinges on those little phrases "in our image" and "according to our likeness." Commentator Derek Kidner writes about Genesis 1:26, "At a single stroke it imprints on the mind the central truth about us. The words *image* and *likeness* reinforce one another."[1] We were made in his image, made to be like God, reflections of the divine formed to show the world what God is like.

How We "Image" God

What does it mean to be made according to God's likeness? How do we "image" him? It means we were built to represent God, to embody his love, beauty, and goodness. We were created to act like and look like him, even in our finite bodies. We were to be little signposts that walk throughout the world advertising God's goodness, showing off his glory, mirroring his beauty. None of this means that we *are* God. We don't rule like he does; we don't have his level of authority. We serve only as his representatives. Though there are many ways in which we image or reflect God, the two we find predominantly in the Scriptures are those of role and relationship.

First, we image God in our role. We go about our days, tackling work projects and establishing homes, planting gardens and training puppies. We act like little kings and queens, exercising authority over creation. God is the ultimate authority, the greatest King, and we imitate him when we rule our small slices of his world. We do so in lots of ways, from raising green peppers in our backyards to harnessing the power of electrons to provide energy for a city. All these actions are those of ruling or managing the world. Anthony Hoekema, theologian, writes, "Man is called by God to develop all the potentialities found in nature and in humankind as a whole. He must seek to develop not only agriculture, horticulture, and animal husbandry, but also science, technology, and art. In other words, we have here what is often called the cultural mandate: the command to develop a God-glorifying culture."[2]

God commanded Adam and Eve, our first parents, to rule in this way. He told them in Genesis 1:28, "Be fruitful, multiply, fill the earth, and subdue it. Rule the fish of the sea, the birds of the sky, and every creature that crawls on the earth." The Creator himself told his image bearers to act like him in ruling over everything he had made. He put us together in such a way that we want to do just that. We create and command naturally, like our God. We come to a messy pile of clothes and create order by folding them. We imagine houses for ourselves with wide porches and lovely paint colors and then build them. We tame the weeds in our backyard and plant flower gardens. We have children and nurture and train them to live in this world. Why do we do these things? Because we mirror our God, who creates and commands.

This compulsion to design, shape, and build is a pre-fall reality. We do not work because sin entered the world. We work because God made us to work; we are like God in that way. Humanity was told to work, to multiply, and to rule the earth before Eve ate the fruit (Gen. 1:28; 2:15). Work is not a post-fall but a pre-fall activity, and it is good. Shaping the world is a fundamental part of who we are as humans. We build and create not just to make a living but because we're made to do so. This is how we image God as humans.

Second, we image God in our relationships. We were made to live in constant relationship to God and others. This is not a result of the fall but is baked into our humanity. With God our relationship is always dependent, as a small child depends on a parent. Adam lived in the garden in total reliance on God. His every breath was supplied by

God. His food was grown by God. His purpose, to work and watch over the garden of Eden (Gen. 2:15), was supplied by God. Even his limits were given by God. Genesis 2:16b–17 reads, "You are free to eat from any tree of the garden, but you must not eat from the tree of the knowledge of good and evil, for on the day you eat from it, you will certainly die." God handed Adam the responsibility of tending the entire garden, except for one tree. There he drew the line and expected Adam to live contentedly, trusting God with the boundaries he had designed for him.

We still live in this kind of relationship with God. We are dependent children, looking to our father for food, purpose, and limits. We work in his world, tending to resources and people that are actually his, stewarding time and money that he first gave us. We rely on him for our every breath, our strength, and our wisdom. We come to the end of our fragile selves and depend on him to sustain us from hour to hour. This is no mistake; it's by design. Dependence on God is not weakness but the intention of our Maker. This is where we flourish and find contentment. We are most human when we rely on God.

God Alone Isn't Enough

But God isn't the only one we need. Our need for other humans is also pre-fall. While living in the perfection of the garden, Adam was deemed to be in need of someone else. God said in Genesis 2:18, "It is not good for the man to be alone. I will make a helper corresponding to him." The garden was good. And Adam was good. But Adam existing alone, even with God, was "not good." And so God made a companion for Adam. Our need for other people, our everyday dependence on other humans is not weakness or sin. Having other people in our lives is essential to our humanity. God purposely built into our DNA the necessity of others for both survival and happiness. Our love of or need for others does not point to a lack of love for God. It points to the fact that we're human.

When we live in fellowship or community with others, we act like the God who made us. God is a relational being, existing from all eternity in the Trinity. God has always lived in a community in that sense. Because he is a relational being, so are we. Again Hoekema helps us: "In this way human beings reflect God, who exists not as a solitary being but as a being in fellowship . . . as that between the Father, the Son, and the Holy Spirit."[3] Our fellowship with others points to God's fellowship within himself.

God's Design for Our Hearts

David talks about God's creation of our hearts in Psalm 139:13. He writes, "For it was you who created my inward parts." The phrase translated "inward parts" is the Hebrew word referring to the center of emotion and affection. God formed our innermost hearts, with all their capacity for devotion and loyalty.

God could have created humans as little puppets with no ability to love or hate, heal or damage. He could have made robotic minions who silently did his bidding. But in a most shocking act, God gave us free will and the ability to worship or reject him. He gave us choice, agency, and power to move about the world as we please. He put us together with the ability to feel a massive spectrum of emotions, from delight to despair, envy to excitement, and everything in between. He assembled us with the need to worship someone or something. In other words, he didn't give us a hollow, machine-like interior. He gave us a center of emotion and affection.

Emotion and affection for what? As Creator, God calls us to worship him alone. He commands us to love him above all and then to love the things he loves. All the affections we hold in our hearts that mirror God's affections are to be spent on things and people he cares about. For example, we are to care for his beautiful world, love our families, and advocate for the helpless and oppressed. He wants us to be grieved by idolatry (Exod. 32:19; Acts 17:16), intolerant of injustice (Lev. 19:15; Ps. 82:2), joyful with those who celebrate

(Rom. 12:15), full of compassion for those who suffer (Ps. 112:4; 2 Cor. 1:4), and brimming with love toward all (1 Thess. 3:12). Our massive capacity for emotion is to be spent for the good of others and for the good of creation.

God's Design for Our Bodies

I (Christine) am at the age now where when I walk into a room, about six times out of ten I can't remember why I'm there. The only life I've ever known is one with a body that malfunctions. Even at a much younger age, I lived with the decay and failure of my physical body. But Adam and Eve did not. How did their bodies work? What was it like to live in a physical body that wasn't affected by sin?

Here is where we see God, the Master Designer, exhibit his brilliance in his creation of the human body. In particular, the brain is unparalleled in its design. It weighs about three pounds (think large pineapple) in the average adult. It's complex, intricate, and runs everything from the neck down. It does so both with and without our conscious control. It communicates using tiny nerve cells or neurons to transmit energy and information.

To do all this communicating, the average adult brain contains approximately 100 billion neurons. Information can run between neurons at speeds of up to 250 mph.[4] (Think Formula 1 car fast.) This incredibly large network of neurons makes up our nervous system, which controls everything from muscles to organs to the brain itself.

Between our billions of neurons travel chemical messengers called "neurotransmitters." These cause electrical signals and allow communication across our entire nervous system. (Imagine high-speed trains zipping across your brain in all directions.) Scientists have discovered at least one hundred different types of these fascinating messengers, some of whose main job is to influence our mood.

Here are just three of the neurotransmitters God made for our brains that enable us to function and feel well:

Dopamine brings feelings of pleasure and motivation. It's released by our brains during activities we love. You may have heard of the dopamine "hit" people receive when their social media post gets "liked." Laughing, sex, and completing tasks also cause a release of dopamine. God included this reward system in our brain chemistry for doing these things. We come back and do them again and again because they feel good.

Endorphins produce euphoria and are released when your body feels pain or stress. They're released to reduce your pain and stress and improve your mood overall. Exercise, food, laughter, sex, and massage can all produce endorphins. Runners talk about a "runner's high" they experience at some point during or after exercise. That high comes from the endorphins' effect on their brain. Extended periods of deep belly laughs can also release endorphins.

Serotonin regulates mood. It's often called the "feel good" neurotransmitter and is produced by your brain and gut. Serotonin helps you focus, keeps you stable and calm, controls appetite and digestion, and affects how long and how well you sleep. Most of us look forward to sunny days and enjoy being outside in the sunshine. This is reinforced by our brains, since sunlight stimulates the parts of our retina that then cue our brain to produce serotonin. God has wired our brains in such a way that sunshine literally makes us feel good.

After a long and arduous week or month, have you ever finally gotten one of those days you worked hard on a meaningful task, enjoyed some outdoor time in the sunshine, and laughed with old friends at dinner? There's a reason that kind of day feels different from the rest. And that's because God created dopamine, endorphins, and serotonin for our pleasure and well-being so that we might be internally and biologically rewarded for keeping our bodies within his good design. And that's only three out of a whole assortment of neurotransmitters! In his elaborate arrangement of our bodies, he provided these powerful chemical messengers to keep us regulated—to help us manage our thoughts, emotions, and behaviors. Good neurotransmitter levels help keep us happy and calm.

Keeping Us Regulated

Remember that all the nerve cells or "neurons" in our entire body together make up our nervous system. That system is always processing energy and information to help us respond to what's inside us and what's around us. It acts like a giant switchboard for the body, helping all of our senses talk to our brain. One portion of that system, the autonomic nervous system, controls and regulates involuntary body functions like breathing and digestion. God created our bodies to respond to certain stimuli automatically, without us even having to think about them. We sweat, cry, and secrete hormones, among other things, all without consciously telling our bodies to do so.

Consider how helpful these processes are in keeping us regulated. If you're sitting on the couch in your living room and notice a large spider crawling across the floor, your eyes notice something that may feel dangerous and communicate through your sympathetic nervous system to your brain. Your body then reacts to this perceived threat with a fight, flight, freeze, or fawn reaction. Your prefrontal cortex then begins to work through choices you have at this moment. Do you get up? Stay still? Scream for help? At that particular moment, you realize that it is not, in fact, a spider, but a strangely shaped hairball from your dog's fur being blown by the fan. As you figure out you're not in danger, your parasympathetic nervous system begins to calm you.

Neurotransmitters help you shift between a state of calm and a state of stress multiple times a day. When you sense danger (*Is that a spider?*), part of your nervous system increases your heart rate. It helps your brain focus and increases your alertness so you can figure out what in the world that thing on the floor is. When the danger has passed (*Whew, it's just a furball.*), the parasympathetic nervous system slows your heart rate back down. Fun fact: If you take a long, slow, deep breath, calming signals are sent to the brain, activating this part of the nervous system, bringing you to calm. What an amazing body our God designed to enable us to navigate the world around us!

Scripture talks not only about God's creating the inner heart but also about God's construction of our entire physical body (Gen. 2:9, 22; Ps. 139:13–16; Job 10:11; Eccles. 11:5; Isa. 44:24; Jer. 1:5). God thought up and built every neuron, chemical messenger, and brain system. He knit together every human's nervous system. The goodness and beauty of your body is a reason to praise God. Your body's ability to sleep and digest food, regulate itself and grow—those abilities were not given by accident. They were being woven into you before anyone even knew you existed.

Hearts, Bodies, and Relationships

Think back to our discussion of the way we image God, in role and relationship. Our emotions and the nervous system that influences them are part of our relationships with God and other people. We reflect God when we feel things deeply. We act like God when we experience joy at the birth of a baby, happiness when we see a beautiful sunset, or satisfaction from finishing a project. We image God when we love our spouse, enjoy our children, and laugh with our friends. We also image him when we sense sadness at a friend's death and anger at abuse of other humans. Emotions are a good gift that enable us to experience this world in its fullness.

What does God's creation of our feeling hearts and wonderful bodies mean for our relationship with him? It means, believe it or not, that God desires to be close to you. He spent thousands of years and an endless amount of energy pursuing his people, including you. He chose a man (Abram) and then a nation (Israel) to represent himself to the world. He promised to be with those who were loyal to him. And as his people grew, he said over and over to his Old Testament people that he will be their God and they will be his people (Gen. 17:7; Exod. 6:7; Ezek. 34:24, 28; Jer. 7:23; 30:33; 31:33). This desire of God's heart does not end in the Old Testament. In the incarnation of Christ, he makes good on this. In the person of Jesus, God came very near, walking around in our skin, dwelling with humanity in the flesh, and experiencing all the things we do. And even after his death, burial, resurrection, and ascension, the same goal is still making its way to full fruition. He has promised to return once more and be with us in the most intimate way, face-to-face, in the new heavens and the new earth where "God's dwelling is with humanity, and he will live with them. They will be his peoples, and God himself will be with them and will be their God" (Rev. 21:3). Being with us was always God's intention. He still wants connection and intimacy with his people, with *you*, even now.

What does God's careful creation of hearts and bodies mean for relationships between people? God made clear that we were meant to live in relationship with others. (Recall the creation of Eve in Genesis 2:22.) The way he blesses and reinforces those relationships, even physiologically, is truly remarkable. For example, the hormone oxytocin is produced in the brain and released into the bloodstream after a twenty-second hug, strengthening bonds in marriage, parenting, and friendship. It's released during sex and breastfeeding and is even sometimes called the "cuddle chemical." Our brains benefit from oxytocin when we offer a gesture of kindness, hospitality, or help toward others.[5] God built into our systems both the need and reward for being close to other people.

But wait, there's more! As he created our bodies, God reinforced the bonds between humans in an even deeper way. The bond formed between a baby and a parent is called "attachment" by those in the world of child development. But that attachment or lack thereof affects the way we relate to others long after we've grown out of the baby years. God created a wonderful self-perpetuating cycle with babies and their caregivers to train little humans to trust others. Through thousands of repetitions of the "I cry, you come" pattern, the baby begins to form neural pathways in her brain that teach her other people are trustworthy and will help her. This attachment is eventually also gained in other healthy relationships with friends, spouses, and her own children. Just as we're designed to attach to others, so God has designed us to attach to him.

Anthony Hoekema wrote, "Man cannot be truly human apart from others."[6] Our DNA programs us to need others from birth. We are built to rely on and respond to caregivers and friends, children and parents, even coworkers and neighbors. A large part of our flourishing as people depends on healthy, reciprocal relationships that are fortified with genuine bonds that are upheld not just emotionally but biologically and hormonally. This was always God's plan, to bind us together as humans as we live in interdependent relationships.

You and I have lived for so long with hearts and bodies tainted by sin that we almost can't imagine what life looked like before sin and death entered the world. But God's plan for his first children included a perfect, joyful, worshipful relationship with him where they enjoyed his love and played, worked, and rested in his beautiful creation. Adam and Eve felt seen, heard, safe, treasured, and cherished by God and by each other. Their hearts and bodies responded to God and others without shame or guilt, fear or sadness (Gen. 2:25). They focused when they wanted to without fogginess or distraction, intrusive thoughts or dread. They were bonded to the Lord and to each other without any need to protect from threats or harm. This kind of life may seem like a pipe dream, but it was reality for our first parents for a little while. And as we'll see in chapter 10, it will be for us one day as well.

Questions for Reflection

1. In what way do we image God that surprises you most? Why?

2. What is your reaction to God's design for our hearts and his desire to be close to us?

3. What was the most interesting fact you learned about the design of the human body? Why?

4. What new ideas about our relationship with God and others did you learn? How does that idea impact the way you think about your own relationships?

Chapter 3

Not the Way It's Supposed to Be

Therefore, just as sin entered the world through one man, and death through sin, and in this way death came to all people. . . . Death reigned from the time of Adam. . . . But the gift is not like the trespass. For if the many died by the trespass of the one man, how much more did God's grace and the gift that came by the grace of the one man, Jesus Christ, overflow to the many! . . . For if, by the trespass of the one man, death reigned through that one man, how much more will those who receive God's abundant provision of grace and of the gift of righteousness reign in life through the one man, Jesus Christ!

Romans 5:12, 14–15, 17 NIV

If you've been around the church for a while, you've listened to a sermon at some point referring directly or indirectly to Genesis 3. It's a foundational passage about humans and their decisions. But what does this ancient story have to do with our present problem of living with anxiety and depression? Is it connected at all?

Indeed. What happened in the garden of Eden was the starting point not only for sin and rebellion but also for anxiety, depression, and every other type of suffering humans endure. If you've experienced these debilitating conditions, please know you're not alone, and you're certainly not the first.

The first and second chapters of Genesis record God's creation of the earth, man, woman, and all things. Chapter 3 begins with these ominous words: "Now the serpent was the most cunning of all the wild animals that the LORD God had made." The beautiful, precisely ordered world was about to be wrecked by the temptation of one of God's creatures and the sin of another. The serpent lied to Eve, convincing her that God had sinister motives for holding back a part of the garden from her.

The serpent began to sow the seeds of distrust in Eve's heart and mind with his first question: "Did God really say, 'You can't eat from any tree in the garden'?" She responded, "We may eat the fruit from the trees in the garden. But about the fruit of the tree in the middle of the garden, God said, 'You must not eat it or touch it, or you will die.'"

The serpent's response continued to undermine Eve's trust in God, accusing God of speaking falsely: "You will not surely die. For God knows that when you eat of it your eyes will be opened, and you will be like God, knowing good and evil" (vv. 4–5 ESV). His words were partially true and partially false. Would Eve die? Yes, eventually.

One day in the future her heart would cease to beat, her breathing would stop, and she would return to the ground. Would she immediately die? No, not immediately. But in that one moment, disease and decay entered the world because of her decision. The slow creep toward death began. Her eyes were opened, as Satan predicted, and she did know something about the good God had made and the evil distortion of it. But she was not, and would never be, on par with God in terms of omniscience, even though the serpent promised she would.

The Devastation Begins

We're not told how long Adam and Eve lived happily in the garden—in a blissful state where they were "naked, yet felt no shame" (Gen. 2:25)—before they fell to the serpent's scheme. But as soon as they ate the fruit, shame entered their world. Genesis 3:7 continues the story: "Then the eyes of both of them were opened, and they knew they were naked; so they sewed fig leaves together and made coverings for themselves." Though they had been naked their entire lives, only after they sinned did they recognize their nakedness and seek to cover themselves. On top of covering themselves up in the sight of God, they also ran away from him in order to hide, further illustrating a sense of separation: "Then the man and his wife heard the sound of the LORD God walking in the garden at the time of the evening breeze, and they hid from the LORD God among the trees of the garden. So the LORD God called out to the man and said to him, 'Where are you?' And he said, 'I heard you in the garden, and I was afraid because I was naked, so I hid'" (Gen. 3:8–10).

What had previously been enjoyed with all the other delights of the garden was suddenly something to be covered, hidden, protected. This was the first indication of the tragic difference in Adam and Eve's formerly perfect world. A barrier to the intimacy they had known with each other and with the Lord had been built because of their choices.

Shame was only the beginning of the countless repercussions of Eve's choice. What was once a relationship of mutual love between the Creator and his created beings became one fraught with confusion and hiding. The next time they met with God, they felt a new emotion—unworthiness.

As the verse above states, Adam and Eve heard God walking in the garden. It was a familiar sound that we can assume previously stirred joy in anticipation of being with their God. Now, instead, they could only think of how they had disobeyed him and of what punishment they would face. Guilt and fear had entered their hearts when they disobeyed God, driving them away from him. The intimate connection between God and his people had been damaged.

The consequences of Adam and Eve's actions extended to their relationship with each other as well. Where there had once been complete trust, respect, and love between the two of them, now blame and suspicion existed. When the Lord asked Adam point blank if he had eaten from the tree from which he commanded them not to eat, Adam blamed his wife: "The woman whom you gave to be with me, she gave me fruit of the tree, and I ate" (Gen. 3:12 ESV). Instead of taking responsibility for his own actions, Adam chose to blame Eve in an effort to save his own reputation. Eve, too, when questioned by the

Lord about her choice, passes the blame along as well: "The serpent deceived me, and I ate" (Gen. 3:13).

The Curse and Its Consequences

God's response was twofold. In mercy, he covered Adam and Eve's nakedness with animal skins (Gen. 3:21)—something far more durable than any self-made fig leaf covering, and something pointing forward to the animal sacrifice system of the Old Testament (and eventually to Christ's sacrifice in the New!).

But we can't miss the other part of what God does in Genesis 3 because it sheds light on another reason difficult, toilsome, and dark experiences are part of human existence post-fall. In response to sin, God curses both the serpent and the ground. The earth itself felt the consequences of Adam and Eve's sin and does to this day. God spoke these harsh words to Adam in Genesis 3:17–19 (ESV):

> Because you have listened to the voice of your wife
> and have eaten of the tree
> of which I commanded you,
> "You shall not eat of it,"
> cursed is the ground because of you;
> in pain you shall eat of it all the days of your life;
> thorns and thistles it shall bring forth for you;
> and you shall eat the plants of the field.
> By the sweat of your face
> you shall eat bread,
> till you return to the ground,
> for out of it you were taken;
> for you are dust,
> and to dust you shall return.

The very dirt had been cursed. What was made to be fruitful, beautiful, and life-giving had been frustrated and stifled. Delicious gifts from God that had once grown without hindrance could only be harvested while working against the thorns and weeds that threatened to choke them out. Everything that came out of and lived in the dirt was affected. Tiny bugs and colorful birds, quick-footed lizards and rough-scaled fishes all felt, and still feel, the weight of the fall. Where there had once been no animosity between certain creatures, now hostility and threats existed. Predators hunted prey, and mothers learned to protect their young from hungry neighbors. What was meant to reflect God's peace and beauty was marred, left to struggle for survival.

In Romans 8:19–22 (ESV), Paul described the state of creation because of sin: "For the creation waits with eager longing for the revealing of the sons of God. For the creation was subjected to futility, not willingly, but because of him who subjected it, in hope that the creation itself will be set free from its bondage to corruption and obtain the freedom of the glory of the children of God. For we know that the whole creation has been groaning together in the pains of childbirth until now."

The creation—the trees, flowers, rivers, and hills—in some way all groan together with humans in our present age. The word Paul uses here describes a collective lament, a grieving of the damage that was done in the world by sin.

If you've ever looked at all of the pain in the world, or even at the pain in your own life, and thought, *Why? What is wrong with this place? Where did all this pain and suffering come from?*, this is the answer you've been looking for. You're still living in a world that groans, laments, and waits for restoration. The tentacles of death and decay have wrapped themselves around the lives of your friends, children, parents, and coworkers. No wonder you feel the ache of things not being the way they were supposed to be.

The Consequences for the Outer Self: Our Bodies

Remember God's words in Genesis 3:19 (ESV): "For you are dust, and to dust you shall return." Adam and Eve's bodies, made in love for satisfying work and joyful intimacy, had begun the slow march toward death. All the intricately created systems and processes made by God for flourishing and health in human bodies were also affected by sin. So much so that in 2 Corinthians 5:2–3 (ESV) Paul writes, "For in this tent we groan, longing to put on our heavenly dwelling, if indeed by putting it on we may not be found naked."

Consider what this means for everyone you know. Everything from their skin to their nervous system to their appendix has been affected. Things don't work as they were intended to work. Hearts created to efficiently pump blood and therefore oxygen around the body have valves that don't open and close correctly. Lungs with intricately formed airways become narrow, making it difficult to breathe. Cells made to replicate for healthy growth instead turn out cancerous cells that invade entire organ systems. Skin created to protect and absorb the sun's warmth is instead damaged by it.

Every bodily system and process—the *material* part of humanity—has been adversely affected by the fall. This implies that everything from Lou Gehrig's disease to Parkinson's is ultimately a result of what Adam and Eve chose. Eczema, arthritis, and diabetes; leukemia, lupus, and high blood pressure; Alzheimer's, anxiety, and depression all exist because of the fall of mankind. Just as every organ and function in the human body were created and declared "good" by God, so each has been marred and contorted by the fall. The bodies that were meant to breathe, walk, and work for eternity instead slowly deteriorate until they are no longer viable. This is the reason Paul calls our bodies "corruptible" in 1 Corinthians 15:53 as he writes, "For this corruptible body must be clothed with incorruptibility, and this mortal body must be clothed with immortality." Our bodies are broken—capable of breakdown and decay in various ways—needing help and restoration.

If we begin to consider all the bodily systems controlled and regulated by our brains, the full impact of the fall begins to dawn on us. Remember that parasympathetic nervous system, which was made to help us breathe and calm down? It's been hijacked. Sometimes, the nervous system gets inflamed and can actually lead to depression.[1] All those beautiful parts of the brain that were created to help you solve problems, build relationships, and prioritize tasks no longer work as they should. The part of our brain that's supposed to regulate us can be sluggish and lead to anxiety.[2] And those neurotransmitters like serotonin, dopamine, and endorphins that were supposed to make us feel good? Now they struggle to do their job every day. Though researchers may disagree about all the causes of anxiety and depression, they all agree that bodily dysfunction is a part of the puzzle. Why does all this matter? Because it's evidence that our bodies didn't make it through the fall unscathed.

All parts of our body haven't completely failed. Some of them still work well while others malfunction. The failures of Adam and Eve in the garden are the reason anxiety and depression exist. If you're looking for ground zero of why anxiety or depression exists in this world, this is it. Because of the sweeping effects of the fall, we've needed categories and labels to describe the impact on our bodies. This is why labels like Parkinson's, depression, or diabetes even exist. We name them in order to understand them and treat them.

The Consequences for the Inner Self: Our Hearts

As if the malfunctioning of humanity's material existence was not enough to cause a struggle, the fall of man also marred the *immaterial* part of our existence. Put differently, we don't just live with bodies that break down, we also live with the waywardness of our hearts. Instead of a heart that is naturally bent toward God and others, the human heart now naturally turns in on itself in stubbornness, self-interest, and pride (Ps. 81:12; Ezek. 3:17; Rom. 2:5). Instead of enlightened hearts of tenderness, we are born with darkened hearts of stone (Ezek. 11:19; 36:26; Rom. 1:21). Instead of healthy hearts that direct us toward God and truth, we are born with sick hearts that deceive us (Jer. 17:9). Our desires, motivations, and imaginations have been tainted by sin, and when those inner realities eventually guide our outer actions, they lead us down dark roads (Eccles. 9:3;

Mark 7:20–23; James 1:14–15). In sum, humanity's great fall into sin did not just result in a compromised outer self but a compromised inner state (Rom. 3:9–12) where people turned away from God and instead "*set up idols in their hearts*" (Ezek. 14:4 NLT, emphasis added).

When we consider all the factors contributing to anxiety and depression, we must not underestimate the impact of our twisted, sinful hearts. For example, because of the way sin distorts our hearts, we often do not trust God when he tells us he loves us and will care for us. Therefore, when difficult situations in our circumstances arise, we can imagine worst-case scenarios in the future instead of allowing God to comfort us with his presence in the present. In another example, we sometimes swat away God's guiding and sovereign hand in any given situation and instead try to reach for the idol of control that has taken up residence in our hearts.

In these attempts to control and shape our lives, we often believe the entire time that we are alone, orphans, uncared for, and unloved—which can produce a high level of anxiety. Or perhaps the sadness and hard things in our lives bring a weariness that seems difficult but comfortable. Reaching for and holding onto the hope God offers takes effort and humility. So we cuddle up in the blanket of our sadness and refuse to risk hoping in what we fear might not come. We can wallow and turn away from God even as he offers his help. These fallen inclinations of the heart are then compounded at times by the brokenness of our bodies in a terrible, synergistic duo.

While we deal with our distorted hearts and bent bodies, we cannot forget another way our inner and outer life is impacted negatively in this world, and that is by Satan. He is the one who twisted God's words and tempted Eve in the first place, and he is still twisting God's words and attempting to lure us away from God, especially when our hearts and bodies find themselves in vulnerable seasons. Satan manufactures all kinds of lies and attacks that use the effects of the fall against us at opportune times (Luke 4:13; 1 Pet. 5:8).

Hurt People Hurt People

The devastation of sin continues in our relationships. Because our hearts and minds are damaged and distorted, we damage others. Relationships were meant to encourage, provide companionship, and multiply joy. But damaged people damage people—sometimes by accident and sometimes on purpose. Physical, sexual, spiritual, or verbal abuse can show up in relationships that are supposed to be places of nurture and safety. And, because of the power of relationships between humans, we can be seriously injured by people and experiences.

The book of James explains this dynamic well. It reveals that what is going on deep inside spills out onto others in ways that damage our surrounding relationships. Look at the damage we do to one another when we get yanked around by our own sinful hearts. In James 4:1–2 we read: "What is the source of wars and fights among you? Don't they come from your passions that wage war within you? You desire and do not have. You murder and covet and cannot obtain. You fight and wage war." The source of the battles—and much of the damage done—in your outer relationships is often caused by problems within your own inner self. People who are hurt on the inside will hurt others on the outside. The implications of this can touch every area of our lives and is clinically called "trauma."

You've probably noticed that trauma has endless definitions these days, and on top of that, you've likely seen many quasi-professionals (or sometimes just self-proclaimed coaches) throwing around the term haphazardly. This can understandably lead Christians to frustration, tempting them to throw the term out altogether since it's now often seen as self-help jargon with no real meaning. However, we commend this agreed-upon definition for trauma, used in clinical environments by properly trained, credentialed counselors: "Any disturbing experience that results in significant fear, helplessness, dissociation, confusion, or other disruptive feelings intense enough to have a long-lasting negative effect on a person's attitudes, behavior, and other aspects of functioning. Traumatic events include those caused by human behavior (e.g., rape, war, industrial accidents) as well as by nature (e.g., earthquakes) and often challenge an individual's view of the world as a just, safe, and predictable place."[3]

Volumes of books have been written about trauma and its effects on human flourishing. We can only briefly touch on it here, but suffice to say that while the concept of trauma can be poorly used in certain ways, it is, many times, a genuine form of suffering. In fact, it is often the primary factor that causes someone to struggle with anxiety or depression. Other times a person's trauma does not cause anxiety and depression but exacerbates each, deepening the impact on daily functioning. Either way, the devastating effects of trauma have their roots in the fall of man.

The God Who Let Us Fall

Reading through Genesis 1–2 provides a wide and wonderful view of God's creativity. We watch as a master painter colors the earth with varying degrees of green, layering different species together in perfect cooperation. We imagine days of pleasure filled with the naming of cockatoos, bullfrogs, and antelopes. But when the scene takes a dark turn, who is to blame?

Wasn't it God who allowed the two humans in his garden to exercise their power of choice? Did he not give them the ability to decide whom they would listen to? If God gave Adam and Eve real freedom to choose, he allowed them to make a choice that led to generations of pain and death. In the specific context of mental health, Adam and Eve's choice ultimately led to suffering for millions of people. Some of us struggle to get out of bed and make a living. Some wrestle in relationships, always worried about rejection. Others find it hard to maintain their bodies and home. Adam and Eve's choice leaves us all struggling to enjoy God and his good gifts. *Why would God allow such freedom if devastation was the end result?*

God and Suffering

Why does God allow suffering? While we do not have the space for a full explanation of such a tender subject here, a few things can be shared about suffering in our consideration of mental health.

Depression and anxiety are a form of suffering. Anyone who has lived through a bout of either can tell you they bring misery. Many who struggle with chronic anxiety have to battle not only their own thoughts but also shame and frustration. They're often misunderstood by those around them who may experience them as high-strung and as unable to "just not worry" or "calm down." Those who live with depression feel the crippling weight of a sadness they cannot explain. They lack energy or motivation to do even the most basic things, and then they also experience the frustration of others who label them as apathetic.

First, *God is not callous to our pain.* Throughout Scripture, we read story after story of God hearing and responding to his people's needs. Exodus 1–2 tell the story of the nation of Israel, God's people, in Egypt, oppressed and enslaved by the Egyptians. While their numbers swelled and Pharaoh grew worried enough about their power to order the Hebrew midwives to kill newborn boys, God was working a plan to save all of Israel.

The Hebrew baby Moses was pulled out of the water and grew to know the oppression of his people. He fled to the land of Midian, where he married the daughter of a priest and attempted to begin a new life and forget about his complicated past. But God had not forgotten the people Moses left behind.

In Exodus 2:23–25 (ESV) we read these words: "During those many days the king of Egypt died, and the people of Israel groaned because of their slavery and cried out for help. Their cry for rescue from slavery came up to God. And God heard their groaning, and God remembered his covenant with Abraham, with Isaac, and with Jacob. God saw the people of Israel—and God knew."

God heard, God remembered, God saw, and God knew. And then God called Moses in the burning bush to return to Egypt and help free Israel. In the great Exodus, God sent ten plagues to convince Pharaoh to let his people leave, parted the Red Sea, and fed two million people with manna in the desert—all because he heard their cry and acted in love to rescue them. God was not callous to the pain of his people in Egypt.

Ah, you might say, but that is the epic story of Israel. What about individuals? Is their pain worth his time? Let's consider Hannah.

In 1 Samuel 1, we find Hannah, a barren Israelite, who was mistreated by her sister-wife and misunderstood by her husband. She lived through years of infertility in a culture that granted women importance based on the number of children they produced. Hannah poured her heart out to the Lord, and he heard her prayer, eventually granting her a baby boy, whom she named Samuel, which means "the Lord hears." She recognized that even though neither her husband nor her husband's cruel second wife could understand her, the Lord could. God was not callous to Hannah's pain.

Walking through the Bible in this way, we find the stories of Elijah the prophet, David the king, Jonathan the friend, and Deborah the judge. If we keep going, we meet Mary the virgin mother, Luke the physician and disciple, Peter the apostle, Paul the missionary and pastor, and John the Gospel writer. All of these and many people in between tell stories of God's loving intervention and salvation when they were in many types of pain. God was not callous to these dear children's pain. He is not callous to ours, either.

Second, *God responds to our pain by entering into it.* The second person of the Trinity, the Son of God, has existed for all eternity. He was content to live in the stunning beauty of heaven and the perfect intimacy of the Godhead. But he intentionally entered our pain out of love and compassion. He took on flesh and came down, cloaking his power in humanity. He took up residence in the womb of a voiceless, powerless teenage girl and was born into poverty. He lived an ordinary life supporting his brothers and sisters by working with his hands, all the while submitting to sinful parents. He continued his downward movement as he ministered for three years with confused and sleepy disciples around Judea and Galilee. He healed the sick, raised the dead, and taught about the kingdom of God.

After being falsely accused, he was taken into custody by the Roman state and crucified as a criminal. By entering into a frail human body, he did more than just care about our pain; he understood it for himself. As Hebrews says, Jesus purposefully decided "to be like his brothers and sisters in every way" (Heb. 2:17). "In every way" includes one major way that we endure the daily experience of being human, and that is suffering. Indeed, "since he himself has suffered when he was tempted, he is able to help those who are tempted" (Heb. 2:18). Jesus's goal in suffering was forgiveness of sin, yes. But it was also to sympathize with, identify with, and help those who face their own sufferings and temptations in this life. "For we do not have a high priest who is unable to sympathize with our weaknesses, but one who has been tempted in every way as we are, yet without sin" (Heb. 4:15).

God's Answer to Our Pain

What is God's response to our pain? He sent Jesus to do something about it.

Jesus always moved toward those in pain. His ministry was often characterized by noticing and having compassion on the people others walked past. He reached out his hand and touched the suffering leper in Matthew 8. He spoke to and delivered the man in the Gerasenes from his many demons in Luke 8.

In Luke's Gospel, Jesus shows compassion to hurting women: the widow of Nain in Luke 7 who also lost her son, the bleeding woman in Luke 8 whom no one noticed, and Mary and Martha in Luke 10 who joined him as partners in ministry. He empathized and emoted with all of them. He is not only the Man of Sorrows (Isa. 53:3); he's the man who *shares* sorrows with those who need help carrying the burden (Matt. 11:28).

Though we still live with the damages of the fall, the pain we endure while here on earth is not the end of the story. Healing is coming, total healing. Right now, healing may come through doctors, counselors, or physical therapists. Or healing may not come until the new heavens and the new earth. In the meantime, we may be sure, God is not callous to our pain. In giving his own Son as a substitute for us, he attended to our pain, and he made provision to one day eliminate forever the source of all suffering. In the person of Christ, God knew our pain by entering into it.

Questions for Reflection

1. What detail about the story of Genesis 3 stood out to you more than it has in the past?

2. What did you learn about the effects of the fall on our bodies? On our hearts? What about that surprised you?

3. Where have you noticed the effects of the fall the most on your body? On your heart? How has this impacted your life?

4. What did you learn about God's presence in our pain? When have you found this to be true?

Chapter 4

Anxious with Anxiety

"When my anxious thoughts multiply within me, Your comfort delights my soul."

Psalm 94:19 NASB

This wasn't the first time I (Hope) felt it, but it was the first time I realized that this wasn't normal. The year was 2002, and I was driving home from one of my first jobs after college as a case manager at an alternative school for at-risk youth in the suburbs of Philadelphia. Though it was only 4:30 p.m., it was pitch-black because it was winter. A wave of panic came over my whole body so intensely that I had to pull the car over and take my jacket off, feeling claustrophobic. I felt like I was coming out of my skin and had no idea what was happening to me. Was my jacket too tight? Why couldn't I drive in it? I was confused by my sheer panic over what felt like a minor situation. It wasn't until weeks later that I landed in a therapist's office. She told me I had anxiety. "What does that mean? Will it go away? Who can I tell about this?" Little did I know the journey that awaited me.

It didn't take long for me to realize I wasn't the only one dealing with this. Approximately 19 percent of Americans have some type of anxiety disorder.[1] I (Hope) have sat for years in my counseling office and heard hundreds of firsthand accounts of anxiety. At first people are usually hesitant to share all the details. They think they sound "crazy," or they're embarrassed by all the ordinary things they're anxious about, from going to the grocery store, to flying on planes, to intrusive thoughts about death, to obsessive worries about what others think about them. But once these thoughts start to force their way to center stage in their lives, they feel so desperate for help that they finally have to talk about their anxiety. They are desperate to understand, desperate to get to the root cause, so they can get some type of relief.

Forever Affected

"I know I wouldn't be anxious if I just believed God's promises more and had more faith." If I had a dollar for every time I've heard that, I would buy you, dear reader, an all-expenses paid trip to the Bahamas. While faith is obviously foundational for dealing with our anxiety, believing that more faith will solve our anxiety problem is an oversimplification. Remember our discussion about sin's entrance into the world in chapter 3? Our bodies, including all their systems and mechanisms, were forever affected by the terrible choice of our first parents. Instead of maintaining constant regulation and calm as they were made to do, our bodies malfunction. Instead of sensing only blessing and shalom from every direction, we now sense various forms of threat. We become riddled with anxiety. Chests tighten with panic. Minds race with worst-case scenarios. Breaths become short and shallow as fear hovers throughout the day.

But our hearts were also affected. Our pre-sin hearts were content with God's provision. Our post-sin hearts hustle and worry that God will not give us enough of what we need. Our pre-sin hearts received God's love like children and basked in his enjoyment of us. Our post-sin hearts fear that God doesn't really love us as he says and won't show up when we are in need. Our pre-sin hearts found great delight in God's being in total control. Our post-sin hearts now jockey for control, doubting God's benevolent reign over our life. We doubt his goodness and worry that he will only expose us to harm.

Because God's image was not obliterated by sin, we are not completely corrupt. We still possess glory, still reflect God's character and beauty simply by existing. But the malfunctioning in our bodies and the corrosion of our hearts touches every system and cell, every motive, thought, and action of our lives in some way.

What Causes Anxiety, and Is It Simply Circumstantial?

Here's an unfortunate news flash: The fall plays out in every human being's life, no exceptions. So, how does this malfunction and corrosion play out in our lives? The full answer includes a thousand different examples and scenarios. But for some people the impact of the fall shows up in part as anxiety, either as a short- or long-term experience. You might be thinking, *Does this mean sin in the world is the only cause of anxiety?* In one word . . . yes, but it's also more complex than that.

People often debate what directly causes anxiety. Depending on whom you ask, you will get a million different answers. As believers we know that anxiety is a result of the fall and that the fall affected three key areas: our hearts, our bodies, and the world. On top of that, we know that Satan uses the effects of the fall against us, especially when we're in a vulnerable season. By way of recap from an earlier chapter (and to add a bit to it):

- Some argue that anxiety is the result of a lack of trust in God and believing he is who he says he is—the problem is our fallen hearts.
- Others argue that anxiety has to do with chemicals (or a lack thereof) in the brain, hormonal imbalances, or a nervous system that cannot regulate itself—the problem is our fallen bodies.
- Still others believe anxiety is a result of traumatic experiences that shape the way we function in the world—the problem is our fallen world.

- Some even say that anxiety is based on your genetics and how your family of origin dealt with anxiety—the problem is all three of the above.[2]
- Other research suggests that adversities, especially in the early years, affect developing brains and the regions of the brain that handle mood—the problem is a fallen world and a fallen brain.[3]
- Some believe anxiety is a spiritual attack—the problem is Satan as he beats down the believer with fear tactics, dread, or catastrophe.

In most cases, anxiety is the result of a combination of the things listed above. Think of it like a three-stranded braid. Our anxiety is actually a "braided" combination of fallen hearts, bodies, and the world/Satan. Different strands represent different root causes, coming together to form the experience of anxiety. It's hard to determine where one starts and the other ends, or which part is the most responsible for the anxiety you are feeling. This takes discernment from the Holy Spirit and conversations with others to tease out. All these things play a role and play off of one another. All three of these components must be considered and weighed with care when trying to understand what is happening in our anxiety. However, the goal of understanding is always to move toward treatment, not to get stuck on this step.

How do I know if my anxiety is just the result of my situation or if it's more than that? What you're asking is, "Is this situational or clinical anxiety?" While most human beings will experience anxious moments or situations in their lives, not every person will have what is called "clinical anxiety." Situational anxiety is usually short-term and goes away after that event is over. It's usually restricted to a particular circumstance. It doesn't interfere with everyday functioning but comes and goes with the stress of life. By contrast, *clinical anxiety* includes persistent and excessive worry that starts to impact daily functioning and continues in this pattern for an extended period. We will continue to unpack what that might look like specifically as we go throughout this chapter.

For now, think about it this way: I might get stressed about taking a test and think about it leading up to testing day. But once the test is over, I'm no longer worried or thinking about the test. This is situational anxiety. However, if I constantly worry about taking the test during the days leading up to it, while taking the test, and even after it, as well as immediately replacing the worry about the test with another fear as soon as the test is over, that is leaning more toward clinical anxiety.

Martha's Anxiety

Let's look at someone's experience of anxiety in the Bible—Martha. Remember Martha? She was close to Jesus as a friend, as were Mary and Lazarus, her sister and brother. Martha loved Jesus and was one of many women who supported his ministry with meals, hospitality, and money as they traveled. Luke 10 gives us insight into Martha's anxiety as she prepared her house and a meal for Jesus and other disciples.

> While they were traveling, he entered a village, and a woman named Martha welcomed him into her home. She had a sister named Mary, who also sat at the Lord's feet and was listening to what he said. But Martha was distracted by her many tasks, and she came up and asked, "Lord, don't you care that my sister has left me to serve alone? So tell her to give me a hand."
>
> The Lord answered her, "Martha, Martha, you are worried and upset about many things, but one thing is necessary. Mary has made the right choice, and it will not be taken away from her." (Luke 10:38–42)

The word Jesus used for *worried*, μεριμνᾷς, is sometimes translated "anxious" and literally means "divided." We could substitute the words *perplexed* or *harassed* for what she was feeling. She was distracted in her mind, pulled in multiple directions. She loved Jesus and wanted to serve him. But she made the work of getting the meal and her house ready her first priority. I think we've all known that feeling just before having people over. Jesus used her sister, Mary, as an example of the "one thing" that was necessary—sitting at his feet and listening.

Bible teachers have used this story to shame thousands of task-oriented, Type A people. Martha has been made into a caricature of a person who cared more about her casserole than about Jesus. We hear phrases about learning to "be a Mary, not a Martha." The truth is, Martha was a Jesus-loving woman who sincerely wanted to serve him and support his mission. And the Scripture makes a point to say Jesus loved her dearly in return (John 11:5). We see examples in Scripture when Martha was serving in the context of food and hospitality without being corrected in any way for it, revealing that a posture of servant-heartedness is, generally speaking, a good thing for a disciple of Christ to display (John 12:2). But in this specific circumstance in Luke 10, she experienced situational anxiety because of all that was on her plate. Martha felt the anxiety we all feel in lots of situations. And for this reason, she's a great example of how Jesus responds to our anxiety.

Notice that Jesus didn't shame Martha. He could have rebuked her in a way that pushed her away from him, dismissing all her efforts as unimportant. Instead, he named her personally and looked past her actions to name her emotional state. He didn't talk to her like a child or a one-dimensional person, scolding her for "doing" instead of "being." (Again, there are other places we see that Martha's "doing" is well-received.)

If we look closely, we see that Jesus isn't frustrated that Martha is in the habit of serving people or welcoming them into her home. He simply points out that she's divided, upset, and fretting about her hospitable work, "anxious and troubled" about it (Luke 10:41 ESV). In other words, the issue is *how she's really doing* underneath all the serving. She's got a chaos-tornado whirling inside of her, and Jesus cares about that. He could have simply received the plates in her hands, but he chooses to show concern about the person spinning them.

Martha is being pulled in many directions by "many things," but Jesus is kind when he reminds her that of these many things, "few things are needed—or indeed only one" (Luke 10:42 NIV). What is this "only one" thing? The wordplay offers some warmth and even humor here. "Mary has chosen the good portion, which will not be taken away from her" (Luke 10:42 ESV). Martha is worried about everyone getting a good portion of food and about Mary taking her fair portion of the work. Jesus is concerned about Martha getting the portion *she* needs in the middle of all this. His words are making it clear that he is her portion—and when Jesus is your portion—when you receive him and "taste and see that the LORD is good" (Ps. 34:8)—it's not like other food. It can't be taken from you.

In this situation, Jesus didn't talk to the outer issues. He talked to Martha's heart. He *saw* her. We can imagine Jesus with an understanding look and a warm tone meeting his disciple's eyes and saying:

"Martha." She stops mid-stride with a plate of bread in one hand and a rag in the other. "Martha." Finally, she looks him in the eye.

"You are distracted and divided about many things. I can see you are worried and upset about everyone receiving their proper portions of work and food." Martha drops her eyes to the floor as he speaks over her.

"There's one portion that matters here, and you're not getting what you need, my daughter. Come and receive your share to partake of instead of making sure everyone else gets theirs. I'm your portion, Martha. Come receive for once."

I imagine it was not a shaming interaction but an inviting one, offering Martha the same place of intimacy with him that Mary had chosen. This was situational anxiety, a moment in time when the circumstances around Martha layered one on top of another until they felt like more than she could handle. She would have worried that the food was not yet ready, that there might not be enough space, that part of the house had not yet been cleaned. Jesus's response was not only to draw attention to this but to reorder Martha's priorities, reminding her that the priority for his disciple is that of intimacy and dependence, of being with and receiving from him.

If one of Jesus's close friends could experience anxiety, how much more can we? And if Jesus was this merciful with Martha as she struggled with situational anxiety, how much more will he comfort those with clinical anxiety who regularly experience this type of suffering?

Is Worry Always Sin?

When people hear about situational anxiety versus clinical anxiety, a typical question arises. But doesn't the Bible tell us not to be anxious? Is anxiety something for which the only solution is to repent and move on?

Well, yes and no. Philippians 4:6–7 reads like this: "Don't worry about anything, but in everything, through prayer and petition with thanksgiving, present your requests to God. And the peace of God, which surpasses all understanding, will guard your hearts and minds in Christ Jesus." Paul is telling the saints in Philippi not to worry—that's right. But not all anxious thoughts are sin.

The word Paul uses for *be anxious*, μεριμνᾶτε, has the idea of being "concerned for."[4] Paul uses this same word when he commends Timothy for being concerned for the welfare of the Philippian Christians: "For I have no one else like-minded who will genuinely care about your interests" (Phil. 2:20). He again uses a form of the same word in 1 Corinthians 12:24–25 when suggesting that believers in the church should care about one another: "Instead, God has put the body together, giving greater honor to the less honorable, so that there would be no division in the body, but that the members would have the same concern for each other." We can be concerned in a good way for other people because we care for them as Jesus has called us to care, not just in an anxious and "divided mind" type of way.

When Is Worry or Anxiety Sin?

So, how do we know when this concern is a good thing and when it's not? In general, when our worries or concerns are combined with doubt about God's care for us, we've moved from useful or healthy concern for someone into sin. It's one thing to be concerned for your aging mother who lives alone. You might check in on her regularly, be sure she has access to an emergency button, or make a plan for a different living situation. It's another thing to live in dread that God will never help you find an appropriate home for her. While all these fears make sense with the current situation, it's the intensity, depth, and your heart's belief about God's help in this moment that are important to weigh and note. It's possible that your worry has turned into sin. No one can judge this in another person. Ask the Spirit to search you and show you if your concern has turned into sin.

Well, doesn't that mean that anxiety is always a sin because anxiety is worry on steroids? Not necessarily. Remember the three-stranded braid we talked about earlier? It depends where the root cause of your anxiety is. While we know that our sinful hearts are always at play, sometimes the effects of the fall on our bodies are more of the root cause when we struggle with anxiety.

But what about the other side? What about when our bodies are the initial cause of anxiety but our hearts are led to sin in response to it? Here's where it gets murky. As a reminder, only the Holy Spirit can discern what is sin and what isn't in our own hearts. This includes when our response to anxiety turns into sin, which can happen. How might this happen? Your body may supply a baseline of anxiety. You might take that initial anxiety and feed it by researching the fear you're focusing on, building a case for your fear. For example, maybe you're scared to fly. Your body responds to the thought of getting on a plane with a tight chest and bouts of diarrhea. But what do you do with it? Do you get on the internet and research plane crashes? Do you feed your brain stories and YouTube videos of flights gone wrong? Out of your mounting fears, do you then lash out at others who decide to fly? This is how we can take the anxiety from our body and let it fuel a decision to sin in order to manage it, only making it worse. (More on how hurting people can hurt others in chapter 3.)

Different Types of Anxiety

We have talked about situational versus clinical anxiety. We've observed Jesus's compassionate response to Martha in a moment of situational anxiety. We have also discussed at what point concern turns into a level of worry that is sinful. But what are some specific clinical types of anxiety? How should Christians think about diagnoses in general?

First, a science-only approach to anxiety might hold a clinical diagnosis as the only complete, full-picture description of what's happening with a person's mental health. For believers, a diagnosis is a helpful tool given to us by a loving God through clinicians, studies, and the psychological world over decades. But it's just one of the tools God has provided. As we will discuss in chapter 6, a clinical diagnosis is only part of a holistic picture needed to help us when we struggle with anxiety. It's a piece of the pie but not the whole pie.

Second, an anti-science or anti-psychology approach to anxiety might focus solely on a person's specific sins or need for character change as the root cause and the only diagnosis needed to move forward in helping them find relief. People in this school of thought might only use admonishment, correction, encouragement, or instruction in godliness as the sole treatment for anxiety. As believers who live embodied lives, we must not ignore our spirituality *or* our physicality. We must consider not only our sin and choices but also how our bodies have been affected by the fall in specific ways that may lead to anxiety. Therefore, our approach to anxiety might be not only a call to repentance in some areas but also a clinical diagnosis for others.

All Truth Is God's Truth

Why can Christians use diagnostic tools invented or facts discovered outside the Bible for their own good? Because all the world belongs to God, and therefore all truth is God's truth. Whatever humans discover about other humans, whether it be the typical growth and development of a child, the way a brain stores a traumatic memory, or the most effective way to help someone overcome their fear of spiders, they're discovering something about God's world.

Augustine, the great theologian of the early church, wrote, "Let every good and true Christian understand that wherever truth may be found, it belongs to his Master."[5] This truth includes not only theological truths like the atonement and the Trinity but also truths about the world in general. Gravity causes an apple to fall to the ground. Water moves throughout our body by osmosis. Leaves use carbon dioxide and water in the process of photosynthesis to make sugar. But also, imminent danger causes fear in humans. Betrayal in marriage damages trust. And sad people need others to help them keep getting out of bed. All these facts describe the physical and moral structures of our world created by God. No matter who names or discovers them, they all belong to him.

Humans made in God's image have been discovering truths about the world and how it works for thousands of years. They've used that knowledge to create tools and practices to help mankind. Christians who use these tools are not failing to trust God. Instead, they're using good gifts given from a God who both has compassion on and understands his creation. For example, a Christian surgeon uses tools that have no relationship to the Bible to mend a broken arm. He might also use a diagnostic protocol written by a non-Christian to diagnose a type of cancer. Or, in another example, a Christian consumer might eat whole wheat bread made by a non-Christian baker. Though the baker is not a believer, he figured out how growing food works in this world—which is a process God built. Surgeon or baker, the principles on which our world works (whether it comes to the human body or earthly soil or otherwise) were created by and belong to God. Unless the protocols, processes, or tools cause the surgeon or consumer to sin (or involve sinful practices), they are not only allowed but are a means of God's bringing relief to his suffering and hungry world.

Before we dive into various types and descriptions of anxiety, one quick word to you, dear reader, especially if you are someone who tends toward anxiety or actively struggles with it. Sometimes just reading diagnoses or descriptions of people's stories or symptoms can feel hard and make your body feel anxious. If that's you, take lots of deep breaths, pray, and take a quick walk or a break from the information as needed. Also, you might feel like you want to read these definitions and jump straight into diagnosing yourself. Slow down. There are more steps to it than that. If you feel like you see yourself in these pages, get a mental health professional or counselor to help you examine whether that's true and what to do next.

Generalized Anxiety Disorder (GAD)

When people think of anxiety, they are usually thinking of generalized anxiety disorder (GAD). GAD looks like someone who has excessive worry most of the time about everything you can imagine in everyday life situations. This person finds it difficult to control their worry, and this isn't a new experience for them. They don't just worry more that week; worry is part of their life day in and day out, with some weeks being worse than others. They also usually have several of the following symptoms: restlessness, feeling on edge, easily fatigued, difficulty concentrating or mind going blank, irritability, muscle tension, and sleep issues.[6] When someone starts to experience this most days for at least six months, they've gone from situational anxiety to clinical anxiety.

This is exactly what I (Hope) was diagnosed with when I had the episode in my car I described at the beginning of this chapter. People who live with this kind of anxiety don't realize that others don't. Part of that is because it's common for people to say they "worry" or "are anxious." But the word *anxiety* doesn't feel or mean the same thing for everyone. For some people it means they're really concerned about an upcoming trip or medical test result. For others it means they will get stuck in their head and worry off and on all day for most days of the week for several months in a row. Their mind is stuck on a hamster wheel of imagining the worst-case scenario. Meanwhile they still have to go to work or cook dinner. It's a lot to balance.

I (Hope) have had clients worry for months on end about unusual physical symptoms in their body, with their minds running off into the worst possibilities imaginable. I have had clients become so anxious they could no longer drive themselves anywhere or walk into stores like Target, which used to be easy for them to do. I have had clients with GAD feel like they are coming out of their skin and literally shake in therapy sessions as they feel debilitated by it. At least half of them have struggled this way since childhood or adolescence.[7] This anxiety is not situational. It doesn't get better when a certain situation changes. It doesn't get better if they just "have more faith" or, in some circles, make passionate declarations in the name of Jesus. These dear people deeply struggle and suffer.

Panic Disorder

I have had so many clients over the years tell me they've experienced such terrible physical symptoms that they ended up in the ER, only to learn they were having a panic attack. Panic attacks can feel terrifying and confusing because the combination of symptoms is so physical. It's like you mixed a bunch of terrible ingredients in a cup and told someone to drink it. The clinical definition for this is panic disorder.

These attacks are any combination of the following symptoms: tightness in chest or shoulders, dizziness, disorientation, rapid heart rate, sweating, feelings of choking, nausea, fear of dying, fear of losing control, chills or heat sensations, shortness of breath, and numbness or tingling.[8] These episodes are like a surge of anxiety and fear running through your body carrying with it both physical and psychological symptoms. Almost no two people experience the same symptoms, but people tend to reexperience their own personal flavor of panic attacks each time they have one. For me they feel like a lightning bolt of anxiety moving from my feet to my head, with a strong need to run out of whatever room I am in, along with tightness in my shoulders.

Here's the real kicker: Once you have a panic attack, you have unlocked a new core fear. If you've suffered from panic attacks, they tend to start a loop in your life that you really don't want to be in. To be diagnosed with this, you must worry for at least a month about having another one and continue to experience panic attacks. You start to worry for months, sometimes years, that you will have another one, which leads to the cycle often described as "anxiety about our anxiety." You may do all kinds of things to avoid the possibility of one happening again. I've had clients who struggle to go to church or drive alone or travel or sometimes even shower because they don't want to return to the place where they experienced such unexpected, inescapable panic. Well-meaning friends try to convince them that they need to be able to go to these places and they should just pray their way through it. While prayer is hugely helpful for all things in life, including panic, this kind of suffering needs to be approached with the complexity it deserves. Prayer is so important, as we'll see later in this chapter, and we want to obey Scripture when it tells us to take our fears and worries straight to the throne of our Father. But prayer can be paired with many other helpful (and God-given) measures to bring relief to sufferers when it comes to panic disorder.

Like other anxiety disorders, there is not just one thing that causes an attack. Although if you have a family member who has panic disorder, you're five times more likely to develop it yourself.[9] Traumatic experiences can greatly contribute to developing panic disorder.[10]

Social Anxiety Disorder (SAD)

Social anxiety disorder (SAD) is another common anxiety disorder. SAD occurs when people have a clinical level of anxiety about social situations, specifically when they think of the way others might judge or observe them. All kinds of scenarios can trigger this reaction—everything from having a conversation, meeting new people, being in a social setting while eating or drinking, giving a speech, or just being observed in general. This goes beyond just shyness or being an introvert, although those things tend to be present among people with SAD.[11] When someone experiences social anxiety, it provokes a level of fear that does not match the true level of threat within the situation they find themselves. This type of fear is not just a one-off, every-now-and-then event. It has to be regularly present and last at least six months to be clinical.[12]

You know that feeling you had when you crossed your middle-school lunchroom and thought everyone was staring at you and laughing? This feels like that, multiplied by a thousand. This anxiety is not just "in your head" because SAD also has intense physical symptoms that go with it. I've had clients who have had to work hard to show up at Bible study, let alone speak there. Some might avoid joining a group of people for a meal for fear that they'll have to eat in front of them. Some clients will go out of their way to avoid interacting with a check-out clerk at a store, calling a doctor back, or speaking to a mechanic. They work hard to avoid social interactions because loneliness feels easier to handle than this level of anxiety.

You might be thinking, *Don't we all feel this way?* Yes, lots of us experience some anxiety in social situations. But the majority of us do not experience it to the degree and severity that makes it diagnosable. While the root causes tend to be a combination of things that we see with other anxieties, they have an added layer of experiencing moments of deep humiliation and embarrassment.

Specific Phobias/Agoraphobia

While there are several more types of clinical anxiety we could talk about, we're just going to cover one more area—specific phobias and agoraphobia. These are separate diagnoses but have enough overlap for our purposes here that we will talk about them together. Both specific phobias and agoraphobia include intense fear and avoidance of specific objects or places. These are accompanied by physical and mental symptoms for at least six months. Specific phobias do just that—they focus on specific objects or situations they fear like flying, snakes, spiders, or needles. On the other hand, agoraphobia includes fear and anxiety of not being able to escape difficult places like public transportation or a crowd. While specific phobias are disruptive, they tend to be less disruptive than agoraphobia, which touches so many day-to-day scenarios. For instance, you can choose not to be around snakes, but it's harder to avoid being in places where you might get trapped like the grocery store.

I, (Hope), have a little bit of both. I've struggled with flying and snakes (specific phobia) and have gone through seasons where being in certain places, crowds, planes, or public transportation led to panic attacks (agoraphobia). Again, it's the intensity and the length of these issues that determines if you are diagnosable. I'm happy to say that all these things have gotten better for me over the years, which we will talk about in chapter 6. But for people who are in the grips of these, they can bring life-altering debilitation. I've had clients who haven't flown in years and have to drive to family events even if they are across the country because their agoraphobia around being "trapped in a plane" is debilitating. I've counseled clients who can't even speak certain words in a session because they're connected to a phobia and trigger a panic attack. These dear brothers and sisters feel like they are navigating a minefield every day not knowing when one of these debilitating objects or situations will strike. They feel like they live in a walking prison.

Comorbid Disorders

Some of you might be thinking that you see more than one of these in yourself. Or you see a combination of one along with depression. Whenever we see more than one mental diagnosis in one person, we're seeing what are called comorbid disorders. Sometimes these conditions are related; sometimes they have nothing to do with each other. But for those believers who struggle with comorbid disorders, they carry a heavy load of suffering and a complex ball of string to untangle.

Mental Symptoms of Anxiety

As you've seen from the list of anxiety disorders, all come with various types of mental symptoms. Even if you don't have an anxiety disorder, you might experience these symptoms. One common example? Racing thoughts. These are thoughts that jump, at a rapid pace, from fear to fear. They're like a bad version of a frog jumping from one lily pad to the next, except the frog is your brain and the lily pads are all your worst fears. They keep going and going. Sometimes instead of jumping from fear to fear, your thoughts will cycle through the same fear over and over and over.

Another example? Imagine an intense hamster working his hamster wheel overtime. This is called ruminating. We can ruminate on anything—the past, the present, negative thoughts, or the replay of a scenario over and over. It can be exhausting and feel hard to get that hamster off the wheel. One more example of a mental symptom of anxiety? Intrusive thoughts. Out of nowhere and unexpectedly, unwanted thoughts or images may pop into your mind. It can feel like you're standing outside when suddenly a bird flies over and defecates on your head, then flies away. You're left with the task of cleaning the excrement off your head while trying to engage with what you were doing before it fell on you. While this is not an exhaustive list of all mental anxiety symptoms, it's a good start.

You might be thinking, *Wait, I experience lots of these things! But I don't think I have clinical anxiety.* Yes, this might be true. And even without a diagnosis, this is still a burdensome pattern in your life that can feel incredibly frustrating and overwhelming. Beloved, God sees you in this place. He knows all of this is going on while you're trying to finish a work task, listen to your toddler tell you a story, or drive a whole carload of kids to youth group. He knows how taxing it is on your brain, your nervous system, and your heart. He wants to care for you as you wrestle with some of the mental symptoms of anxiety.

Physical Symptoms of Anxiety

We have talked about a lot of different types of anxiety and how they can show up physically for you in your body. Now, the tricky part about physical anxiety symptoms is that they can also come from other things. This can make an anxious person not only confused but even more anxious! This is also why it's important to have a conversation with your doctor about your symptoms and let them help you sort them out.

There are many common physical symptoms of anxiety: heart racing, irregular heartbeat, rapid breathing, shortness of breath, muscle tension, chronic stomach issues, tingling sensations, headaches, or lightheadedness. Often all of these are felt along with those mental anxiety symptoms we mentioned before. And like mental anxiety symptoms, you can have them even if you do not completely meet the criteria for an anxiety disorder. Another wild thing about all of this? Every system in your body can manifest symptoms of anxiety, as you can see by this list.

Can you relate to this? Are you experiencing these? It's worth repeating that God sees you in this. He knows how hard this is on you. He promises to meet you in your suffering. And he even gives you biblical examples of those who have struggled similarly in Scripture.

- David wrote in Psalm 6:2–3, "Be gracious to me, LORD, for I am weak; heal me, LORD, for my bones are shaking; my whole being is shaken with terror."
- In Psalm 10:1 we read these words, "LORD, why do you stand so far away? Why do you hide in times of trouble?"

- David wrote in Psalm 13:1–2, "How long, LORD? Will you forget me forever? How long will you hide your face from me? How long will I store up anxious concerns within me, agony in my mind every day?"
- Jesus quoted Psalm 22:1 as he hung on the cross: "My God, my God, why have you abandoned me? Why are you so far from my deliverance and from my words of groaning?" (See Matt. 27:46; Mark 15:34.)
- The same psalm reads later in verse 11, "Don't be far from me, because distress is near and there's no one to help."
- Psalm 94:19 (NASB) speaks further: "When my anxious thoughts multiply within me, Your comfort delights my soul."

All of those words came from just the Psalms alone! If that weren't enough, consider all the anxious expressions of the prophets, both mental and physical:

- Jeremiah's heart rate skyrockets in anguish: "My anguish, my anguish! I writhe in pain! Oh the walls of my heart! My heart is beating wildly; I cannot keep silent, for I hear the sound of the trumpet, the alarm of war" (Jer. 4:19 ESV).
- Isaiah's inner self groans: "Therefore my inner parts moan like a lyre for Moab, and my inmost self for Kir-hareseth" (Isa. 16:11 ESV).
- Habakkuk's whole body responds, inside and out: "I trembled inside when I heard this; my lips quivered with fear. My legs gave way beneath me, and I shook in terror." (Hab. 3:16 NLT)

The list could go on. But hear this: From song writers to kings to prophets in the Bible, it is clear that if you have felt the jolt of anxiety in some physical or mental way, you are not alone.

Anxiety in the Christian Life

How will we know if we're experiencing anxiety like this? What might it look like in our everyday activities? Let's start at home. Anxiety might begin as soon as you open your eyes. You may wake up with tension in your shoulders, a heaviness in your chest, and a low-grade worry about what's planned for the day. It might be difficult to focus on what your children ask as you drive them to school. After dropping them off, you may get stuck on a single fear about someone at work and how they're going to react to a decision you've made. You may imagine them screwing up their face or saying mean words to you over and over. You might have trouble walking by their desk without your heart rate increasing every time you do so.

What about at church? You may have every intention of worshipping and enjoying fellowship but be distracted by multiple anxious thoughts. Perhaps you know an acquaintance doesn't approve of your schooling choices. You know she may be in the service with you, and you can't stop looking for her, just so you know exactly where she is. Maybe you're worried you'll have to use the restroom right in the middle of the sermon and that everyone will watch you walk out and judge you while you do so. You could be sitting next to a friend who knows her Bible better than you and worry the whole time that she'll watch you fumble to find the passage the pastor is reading. Perhaps the music at your church is loud, and you worry each time they start to play that you're not going to be able to stand the noise.

Maybe you've recognized a part of yourself in the descriptions above. Perhaps you've struggled with some type of anxiety but haven't had a name or a category for it. A few thoughts before you move on. First, remember you're dearly loved. God knows your every thought and loves you still. In fact, he provides many tools for relief that we'll discuss later in this book. Second, remember you're not alone. There are people around you who love you and want to help. Third, if one of these diagnoses seems like it might fit, don't stop reading! Find a professional who can help make a clinically sound diagnosis. Whom should you find? We'll talk more about that in chapter 6. And finally, be kind to yourself. Jesus didn't throw Martha out of the Christian community for her anxiety, and he won't do that to you either. Say yes to his invitation to trust him even in this.

Questions for Reflection

1. How did this chapter change your view of anxiety? What did you learn about how anxiety is handled in the Bible?

2. What did you learn about the different types of anxiety? What surprised you?

3. What, if any, physical or mental symptoms of anxiety have you experienced?

4. What part of how anxiety impacts the Christian life stands out to you? Have you or someone you love ever experienced this?

Chapter 5

Depressed About Depression

"From the end of the earth I call to you when my heart is faint. Lead me to the rock that is higher than I."

Psalm 61:2 ESV

I (Christine) sat in the middle of the staircase of my seminary apartment building. I'd willed myself to put one foot in front of the other on the dark carpeted stairs, knowing there was no rational reason to stop. My Greek class was to begin in seven minutes across the small campus. After that was another class, and then work, and then study. I had friends, multiple jobs, professors who cared, interesting papers, and projects to work on. No tragedy had occurred; I was not in the middle of a crisis.

Yet I felt lifeless, flat, gray. I would find myself standing in the shower, unable to motivate myself to wash my hair. Preparing food was an endless chore, and I couldn't enjoy the food once I'd made it. Even being around my favorite people felt like too much. I didn't have the energy it took to attend to their words, to follow their stories, to look them in the face. And so as I reached the halfway point on the way to exit the building that morning, my stamina for the day gave out. It was 7:53 a.m.

I (Christine) am not the only believer walking this road. More than 18 percent of Americans report that they have been diagnosed with depression in their lifetime[1] and the cost of depression in the United States is over $210 billion annually.[2]

I (Hope) have sat for years in my office listening to firsthand accounts of life with depression that ring so similar to Christine's. My clients usually feel a lot of shame that they don't have the "energy" or the "follow-through" they see other people have. The sadness runs deep. It's hard to do almost anything—get out of bed, go to work, cook a meal. The ability to have a hopeful outlook on life feels like a skill they used to have but has since atrophied. Several of them have all this along with thoughts of suicide beckoning to them for some type of relief.

These believers are weighed down and heavy-laden in the truest sense of the word. To use an oversimplification: A person with anxiety is fearful of many things and situations; a depressed person feels deep sadness about many things and situations. Both are desperate for relief, for someone to help them understand why this is happening, and to know what can be done about it.

Forever Affected

"God has given me such a great life. Why am I so sad all the time? He must be so disappointed in me." I (Hope) have heard these heartbreaking words over and over from depressed Christians. They're accounting for sin's effects on their hearts but not remembering its effects on the bodies in which their hearts are housed. Our bodies, with all of their neurons and hormones, cannot escape the far-reaching effects of the fall. Instead of energizing us and supplying consistent motivation and focus for everyday life, our bodies malfunction. We become weighed down with depression. Our limbs become heavy with lifelessness. Our minds are unable to conjure up hope about anything in life; sometimes they despair of life itself. Lungs normally filled with laughter are replaced with deep sighing over the sadness they're carrying.

And, of course, our hearts also fell when sin entered the world. Our pre-sin hearts were full of the joy of knowing God's nearness. Adam and Eve once walked with the Lord through the trees in the garden, enjoying his presence. Our post-sin hearts are full of guilt and shame, and we often reject God's presence and choose to brood in our lonely dark minds instead. Our pre-fall hearts responded to God and others with attention and energy. Our post-fall hearts may turn in on themselves, unmotivated to give thought to much outside of our own misery. Our pre-fall bodies have energy to carry out the tasks of work with joy and delight. Our post-fall bodies have very little gas in the tank and dread the day of work ahead.

Much as they do with anxiety, people often debate the root cause(s) of depression. There are ever-changing theories and ever-evolving answers about this. As believers we know that the root of all bodily breakdown and mental darkness is due to the fall of man and sin's effects. While this might sound like an oversimplified framework, it's important to remember that the fall of man in Genesis 3 was the first domino to fall, starting a chain reaction that led to all kinds of other dominos. This manifests in thousands of different ways and scenarios, resulting in short- or long-term impacts.

As we pointed out in chapter 4, the fall in the garden affected at a minimum three key areas: our hearts, our bodies, and the world/Satan. Similar to the list provided in the anxiety chapter:

- Some argue that depression is the result of a lack of thankfulness for the life God has given us and a failure to believe in his care. The problem is our fallen hearts.
- Others argue that depression has to do with neurotransmitters in the brain not sending and receiving messages the way they should and a flooded nervous system that has shut down and is struggling to regain calm. The problem is our fallen bodies.[3]
- Some say depression is caused by inflammation in the body, impacting and interacting with medical issues already present—also a result of our fallen bodies.[4]
- Others say depression is the direct result of traumatic experiences and their deep, life-altering,

long-lasting impact on humans. The problem is our fallen world.[5]

- Others suggest that poor postnatal care greatly changed how the various brain regions involved in mood and behavior were shaped in the early years. The problem is both a fallen body and a fallen world.[6]
- Many say depression is based on your genetics and how your family of origin dealt with depression. The problem is all three.[7]
- Others say depression is a spiritual attack. The problem is Satan as he beats down the believer with discouragement and despair.

Oftentimes, and much like we said about anxiety, depression can be the result of a combination of a few, or all, of the areas listed above. Remember the three-stranded braid from chapter 4. Depression is a "braided" combination of fallen hearts, bodies, and the world/Satan. Different strands woven together represent different root causes, coming together to lead to depression. These three areas are almost always present and interact with one another, making a combined impact. It can be difficult to tease out which strand is having the greatest impact on a person's depression. Discerning the most likely causes for your depression will take conversations with the Lord and others. To really understand why depression is happening to you, you must examine all three of these areas—fallen hearts, bodies, and the world/Satan—sorting and sifting until you learn what's helpful.

Situational Versus Clinical

Most of us living in a fallen world will experience moments of deep sadness and wrestle with the question, "What is all of life even for?" While these are low moments, they don't necessarily mean that you're experiencing what is called "clinical depression." How do you determine when your depression is in the normal range and when it has gone to another level? What you're trying to discern when you ask this question is whether your depression is situational or clinical. Situational depression is almost always short-term and goes away after whatever event brought it on is over. The circumstance passes and the depression lifts. It also doesn't have a major impact on day-to-day functioning, at least not long-term. On the other hand, clinical depression includes persistent sadness, emptiness, and an irritable mood that affects a person's ability to function for a long period of time. We will continue to build a fuller picture of what that might look like throughout this chapter.

It might be helpful to think about depression this way: Your favorite coworker moves to another city and no longer works with you. You feel sad about this. Over the next few weeks, you start to feel less sad and begin to form new friendships at work. This is situational depression; though the sadness comes, it also leaves. However, if you are constantly sad after your coworker moves months later, and your sadness expands beyond that situation to all kinds of other areas in your life, leaving you feeling hopeless and empty, you might be struggling with clinical depression.

Elijiah's Depression

Even some of God's best-known servants struggled with depression. In 1 Kings 19, the great prophet Elijah had just been used by God to defeat the prophets of Baal in a huge showdown. He was coming off a ministry high. But Jezebel, evil king Ahab's wife, was unmoved by this show of God's power and threatened to kill Elijah. On the surface, it looked as if Elijah's ministry hadn't made a difference. He had just poured his heart out in the most amazing sermon illustration *ever*, and this pagan queen remained coldhearted. Elijah dropped his servant off and traveled a day into the wilderness.

In 1 Kings 19:4–5 we read these words: "He sat down under a broom tree and prayed that he might die. He said, 'I have had enough! Lord, take my life, for I'm no better than my ancestors.' Then he lay down and slept under the broom tree." Elijah came to the conclusion that all of his work, his faithfulness, and his obedience in ministry had not actually moved the needle, and Israel had not returned to Yahweh. In his mind, his efforts were no more effective than previous generations of Israelites, who kept turning away from God. His circumstances led to a place of despair, to a feeling of hopelessness. Elijah was depressed.

Isn't Depression Wrong?

When Christians hear about situational depression versus clinical depression, a typical conundrum arises. Doesn't the Bible command us to rejoice? And if we are to obey those commands, wouldn't depression or despair be a sin against those passages? For example, Philippians 4:4 says, "Rejoice in the Lord always. I will say it again: Rejoice!" and Psalm 5:11 says, "But let all who take refuge in you rejoice; let them shout for joy forever." We're also told multiple times to hope in God and that God expects us to do so. "Let us hold on to the confession of our hope without wavering, since he who promised is faithful" (Heb. 10:23). "The LORD values those who fear him, those who put their hope in his faithful love" (Ps. 147:11).

God tells us to rejoice and to hope. And sometimes when we don't, it's because we've chosen to reject the hope the gospel offers. We may choose instead to wallow in our sadness because it's comfortable and familiar. Real hope is risky and takes energy. On the other hand, sometimes the Bible tells us to be appropriately sad (James 4:9–10; Rom. 12:15b). The world is not the way it was meant to be, and a holy reaction to that reality is lament. The entire book of Lamentations and about one third of the Psalms are lament. God doesn't ask us to stuff our sadness but instead gives us patterns for expressing it to him. We are to direct our complaint to him when we experience the effects of the fall.

Indeed, sorrow is within the range of normal human emotions. Even Jesus lifted up his sadness to God at times (Heb. 5:7).

Furthermore, Jesus told fellow mourners something important: not that they were in sin but that they were, in fact, blessed (Matt. 5:4). Jesus's apostles, particularly Paul, follow suit here. Yes, Paul tells us to rejoice in his letters, but he is also the same man who said, "I have great sorrow and unceasing anguish in my heart," and "I wrote to you out of much affliction and anguish of heart and with many tears" when considering the fate of hard-hearted people (Rom. 9:2; 2 Cor. 2:4 ESV). On top of this, Paul makes space for the category of godly sorrow (2 Cor. 7:10) and tells Christians not to dismiss one another's sadness. Rather, he says that "if one member suffers, all the members suffer with it" (1 Cor. 12:26).

This space for sorrow does not mean the Bible passages about rejoicing and expressing hope are thrown out of the Christian life. Rather, they are held in tension with those on the other side of the emotional spectrum. Christians are allowed to mourn the sorrows of this life, but the key is that in their deep lament, their hearts should not mourn as if they have no hope (1 Thess. 4:13). *Mourning with hope*—both happening at the same time in the human heart—is possible for the Christian.

And remember, it's not just our hearts that fell. Our physical bodies were also terribly affected when sin entered the world. Brains designed to release dopamine and move it through billions of neurons producing pleasure and motivation fail to function properly. Brains and digestive systems that are supposed to release and process serotonin to help buoy us in life malfunction. Chronic pain can make engaging in life next to impossible, darkening our outlook and mood.

Yes, it's wrong that your body and heart sometimes must endure these dysfunctional realities—in the sense that the whole world went wrong after the fall. But this does not mean you are always in the moral wrong for experiencing low seasons. Sometimes a lack of rejoicing is due to sin, and that sin must be rooted out. But other times, certain seasons of sorrow are better understood as an appropriate human experience when living in a fallen world and body.

Different Types of Depression

We have talked about a right response to sadness in the world, how sadness can turn into sin, and the difference between situational and clinical depression. We've observed Elijah's bout with depression. But what are some specific clinical types of depression? And how should Christians think about diagnosing them?

First, a psychology-only approach to depression might hold a clinical diagnosis as the only description of what is happening with a person's mental health. As we discussed with anxiety, believers can use a clinical diagnosis as just one tool in the toolbox of understanding your situation with more clarity. Second, an anti-psychology approach to depression might name a person's specific sins as the reason for their excessive sadness and the only thing needed to move forward in helping them find relief. Then rebuke, teaching, and encouragement may be used to help root out the sin and change their behavior.

As believers in Christ who live with both hearts and bodies tarnished by sin, we know that both our sinful choices and the failure of our bodies can contribute to our depression. Our approach to depression might be biblical encouragement or teaching for some areas and a clinical diagnosis for others. Using both approaches employs a lens that helps us see more clearly and walk toward help and healing.

Remember our discussion about how "all truth is God's truth" in the previous chapter. Christians may use diagnostic tools invented or facts discovered about the world for their own good because all the world belongs to God. Unless a method or practice is sinful or causes us to sin, we should think of these as good gifts from a father who loves us. Michael Lundy wrote in his book about Richard Baxter (a puritan pastor who cared for many struggling with depression), "The Puritans unabashedly took what they could from a variety of sources, holding that all truth was ultimately from God, and that such truth as was revealed to ancient pagans through general revelation could be legitimately recycled, with care, and applied in an explicitly Christian context."[8] We use this same principle today. Just as we might use diagnostic tools developed by an unbeliever to discover high blood pressure, so we may use diagnostic tools to identify depression.

Major Depressive Disorder (MDD)

Typically, when people think of depression, they are thinking of major depressive disorder (MDD). A person with MDD has a depressed mood of sadness and hopelessness. This lasts more than two weeks, most of the day, every day, and is a big change from how they were feeling before their depression. It leads to little interest in most things, especially things they enjoyed before. This person finds it difficult to do routine tasks because of low energy and fatigue. To add insult to injury, on top of their fatigue, they often have sleep issues. Weight loss or gain may show up during this time. Sometimes concentrating or making decisions feels impossible. People usually feel a deep sense of worthlessness. Sometimes feelings of wanting to die will show up with all their other symptoms. Occasionally physical symptoms pop up as well, like body aches and headaches. These feelings aren't related to or caused by grief from a major loss. When these symptoms start to stack up over an extended period, they have gone from situational depression to clinical depression.[9]

I (Christine) was finally diagnosed with MDD during graduate school. Those of us who live with this level of depression watch the world and wonder where everyone gets all their energy. Though other people may talk about being "depressed," not all of them get sucked into the black hole of their minds and can't escape. Some people may feel sad because they've had a falling out with a good friend or their child receives a difficult diagnosis. For others it means they will start with sadness from one situation and slowly add the weight of many other sadnesses until they feel so defeated they can't think of a reason to get out of bed. Their despair may increase to the point that work or even a shower feels impossible, and others must help them with daily tasks. Spouses and children may feel confused by why their wife/husband or mom/dad won't do the things they usually do.

I (Hope) have had clients who are so depressed that they find it hard to leave the house, let alone come to a counseling session. They often cancel at the last minute. Others feel like the hopelessness will never end and cry through the whole session. Some haven't been able to do basic tasks like laundry or dishes for days or weeks, while others have had a hard time finding the energy to run necessary errands. This all makes sense when you consider the fact that MDD is the leading cause of disability in the United States for people ages fifteen to forty-four.[10] This means that saints in our churches with MDD might be having a hard time getting to worship on Sunday morning.

Persistent Depressive Disorder (PDD)

Another common form of depression is persistent depressive disorder or PDD. It packs less of a punch than MDD but hangs around for a really long time. You must have depressive symptoms for over two years to receive a diagnosis. Often this disorder starts in childhood or adolescence, which can make it hard to recognize. It looks like low energy, fatigue, and feelings of hopelessness. It's a lot like MDD but with less intensity. It also has elements of low self-esteem. People with PDD might find it easier to carry on with tasks like work or school. But to understand their struggle, we should imagine them wearing dark tinted glasses that make everything duller.[11]

Most of my (Hope) clients with PDD are hard to spot, both for the client and for me. This type of depression flies just below the radar so it doesn't sound the alarm that MDD does. It's still a major game changer in terms of how these people see life, themselves, and the everyday tasks required to live. I have had clients just drag from day to day for years. They drag themselves out of bed, to work, to the carpool line, to the grocery store, and to evening activities all the while pulling an invisible thirty-pound bag of bricks behind them. They usually can't figure out why they feel "off" or don't seem to be as joyful as others. When functioning this way, your view of self often erodes. While all of us experience this on some level, the daily struggle of this type of depression sets it apart as its own kind of suffering.

Bipolar Disorder

Almost no diagnosis comes with more stigma and confusion than bipolar disorder. While bipolar is not classified under depressive disorders in the DSM, it has a major depression element within it. We will touch just briefly on it, though a much more thorough explanation is needed to understand it.

There are two types of bipolar—I and II. While there is some overlap in symptoms, these two types vary some within themselves. Both, however, have a major depressive episode (similar to what we described for MDD) along with a manic (abnormally elevated, high-energy mood) or hypomanic episode (abnormally elevated mood but not as high as classic mania). People with bipolar will cycle through the mania only to be dropped into a major depression that can last for a long time. Mania can look like high levels of energy or irritability accompanied by all kinds of high-risk behaviors like excessive shopping (lasting at least seven days). Hypomania, found with bipolar II, lasts four days and includes high highs and risky behavior. Saints who struggle with this are taken on an exhausting, disorienting ride by the chemicals in their brain, often damaging people in their wake. This disorder leaves people and their loved ones confused about how to deal with their various behaviors. They may struggle to get the right treatment to prevent the disorder from taking a heavy toll on their families.[12]

I have listened to believers over the years who have been devastated by a bipolar diagnosis. Not only because of the havoc that mania and depression wreak on their lives but also because of cultural phrases used in jest like, "You're acting so bipolar." People who are truly bipolar experience so much shame by these words and can sometimes equate bipolar with being "crazy" and unpredictable. They often feel scared of what their own brain will do. I spend time with my clients finding ways to get support and prepare for mania. We also think about ways to try to prevent a total slide into depression and what to do if that happens.

Seasonal Affective Disorder (SAD)

Around the beginning of November every year, St. Louis turns gray and stays that way until mid-April. There are sunny days, for sure. But most of the time the sky is a light gray, even whitish sometimes. When this happens I (Christine) begin my annual struggle with seasonal affective disorder (SAD). I cannot explain what this does to my energy level. Sometimes I don't realize how low I feel until suddenly a cloud breaks and the sun shines through. It's as if someone has plugged me back in or shot adrenaline into my arm. Suddenly it's going to be okay, I can keep going, there is beauty in the world. It can be a disorienting feeling to go back and forth between sadness and happiness just because of sunshine or the lack of it.

SAD (not to be confused with the other SAD—social anxiety disorder) is the seasonal component of MDD. It's a type of depression that shows up when the days get shorter in the fall and winter. This reduction in daily sunlight can affect how the body makes certain chemical messengers that help with mood. For people with SAD, the continuous loss of sunlight—which happens daily in the winter—makes them feel like someone is draining their battery with no way to recharge it for months. The early sunsets and long nights make the energy supply continue to dwindle and lack of motivation grow. Most of my (Hope) clients who struggle with this dread the winters and feel drop-kicked by daylight saving time, as they say, "Every. Single. Year." Others who are new to a struggle with SAD are confused and shocked by less sunlight having such an effect on their ability to function.[13] I usually prep these clients around October for what is coming, and we strategize about how to get them through the next few months.

Postpartum Depression (PPD)/Premenstrual Dysphoric Disorder (PDD)

Two types of depression affect only women: perinatal depression/postpartum depression (PPD) and premenstrual dysphoric disorder (PMDD). PMDD is like typical PMS (premenstrual syndrome) on steroids! It occurs between ovulation and the start of one's period. Women who struggle with this describe a noticeable increase in mood issues like depression, anxiety, anger, and irritability. If you already struggle with clinical anxiety and depression, PMDD only compounds the effects of these diagnoses. Fun, right? These intense mood increases are often accompanied by the things women typically experience during PMS: bloating, breast tenderness, fatigue, headaches, stomach issues, etc. These all occur in a specific window of the month and resolve once the period starts, only to show up the next month. Women are not being dramatic or exaggerating PMS symptoms when they complain of these symptom levels; this is a real diagnosis with real implications for monthly functioning.[14]

I (Hope) remember a specific client sitting across from me in my office. She'd had a baby three months before but was struggling to function. Tears filled her eyes as she talked about being shocked and confused by her feelings of deep sadness and hopelessness, her constant crying and overwhelm. "I love my baby and wanted to have her. I feel so guilty that I am struggling so badly." She is one of many I have sat with in sessions over the years. Sometimes this starts during pregnancy. Sometimes the symptom is anxiety instead of depression. All the time these women feel shame and fear that somehow this makes them a failure in motherhood. My client wasn't a failure; she had PMDD.

The word *peripartum* means "around childbirth," specifically the end of pregnancy, during labor, and the first few weeks or months after birth. Depression shows up in this window of time for women: 14–23 percent experience this while pregnant and 10–15 percent experience it postpartum.[15] [16] [17] As you can imagine and some of you know, this is such a hard moment for depression to appear. The symptoms of PPD are essentially the same as those of major depression disorder, with one key difference being the timing. While PMDD symptoms must be around for at least two weeks, those symptoms have to fall in the window of pregnancy and after birth, first-year postpartum. Because of that, sometimes symptoms such as having a hard time bonding with the baby or having intrusive thoughts of wanting to harm themselves or the baby can show up as well.[18] You can imagine how ashamed and confused a new mama can feel when they have this new little one that they love so much along with such painful thoughts.

Suicide

One of the most heartbreaking and scary symptoms of depression is that of suicidal ideation, which is having thoughts about ending your own life. Most of us in this life will experience a sense of deep weariness from the suffering, hardship, and traumatic experiences we go through. This often leads to despair, which is grief absent of hope. This can drive Christians to remember our true hope as believers—this earth is not our home. Heaven awaits us, and the pain of life will be behind us.

But for those struggling with the heaviness of depression, thoughts and plans of ending their life can creep in against their will. Of course, this fills them with shame and guilt, knowing that this is not what the Lord wants for them. But their suffering is overwhelming. The effects of the fall pound on them, leading their brain and heart to experience intrusive thoughts or plans of suicide. These thoughts tend to be accompanied by the lies Satan eagerly whispers in their ears as he attempts to convince them that people would be better off without them or that they're a burden. Remember how Peter described Satan's strategy: "Your adversary the devil is prowling around like a roaring lion, looking for anyone he can devour" (1 Pet. 5:8). When believers find themselves in this place, a severe battle with their fallen brain and heart ensues.

When a believer fights against those thoughts, brings them to Jesus, and is honest with trusted people around them, it's a beautiful picture of spiritual strength during a difficult battle. The community should never shame an individual in this place but instead cheer them on and encourage them in their fight for life. It takes an incredible amount of faith to continue to get up day after day when everything in you is telling you to do anything possible to escape. These brothers and sisters are facing a battle most of us will never have to face. They need companions and trench buddies, those willing to take a phone call, pray on the spot, or just show up.

Comorbid Disorders

As was mentioned in the chapter on anxiety, some of you might be thinking that you see more than one of these in yourself. Or you might notice a combination of one of these with a type of anxiety disorder described in chapter 4. Whenever we see more than one mental diagnosis in one person, these are called comorbid disorders. Sometimes these conditions are related; sometimes they have nothing to do with each other. It's not uncommon to see anxiety and depression showing up around each other like old friends. Believers who struggle with comorbid disorders carry a heavy load of suffering that can feel difficult to untangle and figure out.

Mental Symptoms of Depression

As you've seen with all the depressive disorders just identified, each comes with mental symptoms. Even if you don't have a depressive disorder, you still might have experienced or be experiencing some of these symptoms. A common example is a loss of interest in things you once loved. Imagine for a moment a hobby or activity you really enjoy. Just the thought of getting to do it usually gets you excited. Now imagine that bright, joyful, colorful activity drowned in a malaise of dark gray. What once gave you energy now isn't something you can even muster up energy to do. Instead, the hobby feels like a chore. You'd rather just take a nap. This loss of interest usually leads to another symptom: lack of motivation. It's hard to get motivated when life has lost most of its color and shine.

Another example? Feelings like hopelessness and sadness take center stage. Imagine two people named hopelessness and sadness following you around everywhere you go. They're there when you wake up in the morning. They go with you to work. They're there when you're mowing the lawn or paying bills. They're always there when you watch the news. They just hang around constantly. Sometimes if you're at something fun like a birthday party, they might stand in the background. But that's only temporary. Hopelessness and sadness can also lead to other symptoms like numbness. Because when you're sad and hopeless, it doesn't take long for you to slide into numbness to escape. Of course, this isn't an exhaustive list of all the mental depressive symptoms, but these are the big hitters.

You might be thinking, *This all sounds familiar. And I don't think I'm clinically depressed.* You may be exactly right; you may have some of these symptoms but not enough to be diagnosable. And yet, experiencing these things on a regular basis can still be a huge burden in your life. Beloved, this is not lost on God. He knows everything you're experiencing while also trying to finish up expense reports, meet up with a friend, or get your sick dog to the vet. He is present with you as you do life with some of the mental symptoms of depression.

Physical Symptoms of Depression

Physical depression symptoms can show up in the lives of those who are not clinically depressed. Like with most mental symptoms of depression, it's possible for physical symptoms to be caused by disorders or diseases other than depression. That's why it's always important to have a conversation with your doctor about your symptoms and let them help you sort out your symptoms.

People with depression often describe a physical heaviness. It's almost as if someone filled their arms and legs with sand. It can feel hard to move around or experience any lightness or energy. Even the thought of walking or working in any way can feel overwhelming or tiring. This heavy feeling can also lead to two more physical symptoms: flat affect and slow reactivity. Sometimes my depressed clients will pause for several seconds before answering a question. These symptoms create a physical slowness that some people liken to Eeyore, the gray donkey character from Winnie the Pooh.

Depression also has symptoms that can affect a person's ability to think clearly. Brain fog can roll in and make it hard to follow others in conversation and remember what tasks you had just been working on. Sometimes this extends into memory issues and makes it difficult to recall information, which of course makes people feel frustrated and stuck. The brain fog and memory issues make concentration difficult. All these turn normal cognitive tasks into an uphill, exhausting climb. The heaviness and fogginess together can compound into a feeling of being trapped in a body that won't move or doesn't have enough power to keep going.

Do any of these sound familiar? Have you been living with some of these symptoms? Please know that God has compassion for your suffering. He sees your struggle and loves you. As the psalmist writes, "The LORD is near the brokenhearted; he saves those crushed in spirit" (Ps. 34:18). Depression shows up for people in the Bible just like anxiety did and not just for Elijah. The Psalms are full of people crying out to God in their sadness:

- David wrote in Psalm 6:6–7, "I am weary from my groaning; with my tears I dampen my bed and drench my couch every night. My eyes are swollen from grief; they grow old because of all my enemies."
- He wrote again in Psalm 18:4–6, "The ropes of death were wrapped around me; the torrents of destruction terrified me. The ropes of Sheol entangled me; the snares of death confronted me. I called to the LORD in my distress, and I cried to my God for help. From his temple he heard my voice, and my cry to him reached his ears."
- Furthermore, in Psalm 25:16–18, he said: "Turn to me and be gracious to me, for I am alone and afflicted. The distresses of my heart increase; bring me out of my sufferings.

Consider my affliction and trouble, and forgive all my sins."

- Psalm 31:9–10 (NIV) speaks further on how deep sadness plays out in the soul and the body: "Be merciful to me, LORD, for I am in distress; my eyes grow weak with sorrow, my soul and body with grief. My life is consumed by anguish and my years by groaning; my strength fails because of my affliction, and my bones grow weak."

About one-third of the psalms are psalms of lament where the author directed his pain to God.

Similar to what we shared in the previous chapter, all of these words came from just from the Psalms alone! If that weren't enough, there are plenty of other biblical characters who could give voice to what intense sadness feels like.

- Job suffered immense loss and endured severe physical pain, leading to feelings of despair and questioning God (Job 11:16).
- Moses struggled against self-doubt and inadequacy, leading him to question his calling and wish the worst upon himself (Num. 11:15).
- Jeremiah experienced profound sadness and lamentation due to the destruction happening around him (Jer. 20:14–18).
- Hannah poured out deep desperation and cries to God in a season of despair, anguish, and sadness (1 Sam. 1).
- Paul and his companions "don't want you to be unaware, brothers and sisters, of our affliction that took place in Asia. We were completely overwhelmed—beyond our strength—so that we even despaired of life itself" (2 Cor. 1:8).

Depression in the Christian Life

What might depression look like in your everyday life? First, one of your most difficult tasks might be getting out of bed. Within a few seconds of waking up, a depressed person may immediately want to go right back to sleep. But unlike others who are simply still sleepy and hit snooze once or twice, you may legitimately not be able to think of a good reason to get out of bed. The things that usually motivate you or give you joy just aren't enough. Anything more than sleeping for the next several hours might feel like it would take more energy than you have. You may be able to force yourself to help your children get ready for school (or not) but then sit at your desk and stare at your computer screen, unable to focus.

Church might be an extremely difficult place for you, since it's a social place where people greet one another with smiles and hugs, expecting cheery hellos and quick quips about the weekend. Meanwhile you may struggle to force a smile and not have the stamina to make it through four conversations about last night's game or their kid's science project. Singing might be something you just skip altogether. If someone shows you kindness, you might cry and have trouble stopping. Though you may try to listen to the sermon, it might be difficult for you to focus on the pastor's words. Truths about real gospel hope may not penetrate your saddened heart.

Depression can affect any person: moms, dads, sons, daughters, grandparents, friends, neighbors—anyone. It's experienced by pastors, teachers, homemakers, and bankers. While sin's original entrance into the world is always the ultimate root cause, many factors can lead to or add to your depression—personal sin, perhaps, but also plenty of factors beyond that. If you are sad, please know that what you're feeling is a real and an appropriate reaction to the devastation that sin brought into the world. Please also know that if you're experiencing clinical depression of any type, help is available. God has not left us without help in the world, available in a variety of forms. Keep reading; hope is coming.

Questions for Reflection

1. How did this chapter change your view of depression? What did you learn about how depression is handled in the Bible?

2. What did you learn about the different types of depression? What surprised you?

3. What, if any, physical or mental symptoms of depression have you experienced?

4. What from how depression impacts the Christian life stands out to you? Have you or someone you love ever experienced this?

Chapter 6

Attending to Your Anxiety

"The Lord God will help me; therefore I have not been humiliated; therefore I have set my face like flint, and I know I will not be put to shame. The one who vindicates me is near; who will contend with me?... Who has a case against me?... In truth, the Lord God will help me; who will condemn me?"

Isaiah 50:7–9

Sometimes, once we've figured out what's wrong, we're not sure what to do next. We don't know if a diagnosis or struggle with anxiety means we're stuck in the same loop forever or if we should hope for movement and solutions. Here's the good news: Our kind Lord has given us so many ways to push back against the fall in the realm of anxiety.

Hope's Story

I remember being just twenty-three years old and moving across the country for my husband to start seminary in Philadelphia. I'd had a series of panic attacks and a higher level of anxiety than ever before, though I didn't even know the term for what was happening to me. I landed in a psychologist's office who loved the Lord and had great clinical insight. She told me what I was experiencing was anxiety. She wanted me to consider taking medication so she could retrain my mind while I was less heightened and give me helpful tools to fight the anxiety. I remember the awkwardness of sitting in the doctor's office trying to explain to someone I had never met what was happening to me. She recommended a specific medication that was to be taken for at least a year, according to best practice at the time. I remember feeling so desperate that I didn't even question whether it was God honoring to take medication.

I had no idea that those initial moments of addressing my anxiety would start me on a journey I'm still on. I would get off meds only to have to go back on them about every four years. While a baseline level of anxiety was always there, I started to experience a pattern of anxiety episodes. Sometimes a stressful event would kick them off, sometimes not. During these episodes that would last a few weeks to a month, I wouldn't be able to eat much. Sleep was interrupted by panic. I had a hard time working or engaging in much of anything. I would often stay in bed in the mornings because my anxiety was worse at the beginning of the day. I couldn't drive myself to basic things like the store or the doctor. I found it hard to pray and needed people to come and pray over me.

This experience has happened in three different cities over the decades of my life. It's almost like my anxiety cup runs over and my brain sounds the alarm. To return to normal functioning, I go back on meds. I once had a Christian I highly respect ask me, "Why are you resisting the Lord's healing for you by going on medication?" I felt like my motivation was the opposite. God's healing was what I wanted most. I wanted to be free of this painful anxiety pattern. I believed God in his mercy had let some scientist mix this medication up in a lab to push against the fall and what it was doing to my brain. I kissed Jesus's feet over and over again for this kind provision. One day when I was literally coming out of my skin after weeks of panic attacks and not wanting to go on meds again, my pastor deepened my understanding of how to proceed by saying, "Hope, you can't get around the fall and its effects on the brain." That medication, for me, was a gift of common grace. It wasn't the saving grace bought by Jesus's blood. But it was part of the common grace God extends to everyone. That medication pushed against the suffering I was experiencing because of the fall.

I tell you this because many believers experience something like this and don't have a well-developed theological framework for mental illness and how God might allow us to address it. Many of us lack practical theology. We need a combination of theological truth and wisdom to know how to walk these situations out.

Please don't hear what I'm not saying. Not every believer should be on medication for generalized anxiety disorder. My story may not be like your story. But every believer does need a framework to draw from to help them persevere through this particular type of suffering.

What Tools Are Okay to Use?

So, what's a believer to do? What tools are available and appropriate for us to use in our fight against anxiety? Here comes some good news: There are so many! Remember from chapter 4 that all truth is God's truth. Clinicians and researchers who discover truths about our bodies are discovering how God built us and information about *his* world. Therefore, just as we can use diagnostic tools discovered or developed in the world, so also we can use tools and treatment methods from a variety of sources.

But before we even begin listing treatment methods provided by a loving God, first and always we must remember *who* he provided. Jesus is the Great Physician and the Great High Priest who understands our every struggle. Jesus hears every cry and sees each tear. No tool or modality can bring more comfort than the lover of our souls. As you use these tools, invite him into this process with you. Ask for his help. Ask for his insight. Ask him to guide you as the one who created you. Jesus is the one who can empower the change you need.

While treating our anxiety, we need to remember that we are complex people—spiritual and physical beings. Every category of our humanity fell when Adam and Eve sinned. Therefore, all categories must be examined when seeking to push back the effects of sin. We should beware of any quick advice to *only* medicate or *only* repent.

We must be curious about our whole selves and possible sources of anxiety.

Richard Baxter, a seventeenth-century Puritan pastor, wrote about the need for this holistic approach to anxiety with these words: "The rush for 'the right medication' is just as overreaching as have been prior purely psychological formulations, or purely 'spiritual' ones."[1] As we introduce you to helpful tools, some of these will be familiar while others may be new to you. All are tools the believer can use to push back against anxiety. Some are clinical tools. Others are daily practices and spiritual disciplines. All are tools that God, in his mercy, has given believers freedom to use.

Anxiety is often so strong and overwhelming that it can feel like there is no tool powerful enough to get it to subside. That's a lie. Many tools can help lower anxiety, even in the moments when it feels the strongest. But instead of choosing just *one* tool and hoping it will "fix" your anxiety, we often need several. Holistic treatment for mental health does not involve just one thing but many things. A picture might help: Visualize a pie that's been cut into several even slices. Each of these slices represents a different tool to combat anxiety. No one tool will be able to do the trick completely. You will find yourself most likely needing a combination of tools. Different tools have different levels of effectiveness with different people. God has provided all these tools to help you push against the effects of anxiety in your life and bring little bits of redemption in each of these places.

Therapy

Psychotherapy, therapy, or counseling includes regular sessions where you interact with a mental health professional to address a range of topics, including mental health issues. The goal of these interactions is to explore the current problem; understand what historically has led to the situation; discover thoughts, feelings, and triggers involved; and provide strategies to lessen the impact of the problem or interrupt the loop of unhelpful habits. This relationship between a clinician and a client can be a game changer for someone struggling with anxiety. Remember the three-strand braid we discussed in chapters 4 and 5? A therapist or trained Christian counselor is trained to help you sort out those strands and find the roots of your anxiety. They can also give you practical tools to minimize anxiety's effect on your day-to-day life.

Therapists or trained counselors usually fall into two different categories: biblical counselors and secular counselors. Biblical counselors are trained with a biblical worldview and usually do not hold a license like an LPC, LCSW, or doctorate in psychology. A secular counselor will have a master's in counseling or social work, or a PhD in psychology. Once they achieve their degree, they must complete approximately three thousand hours, depending on the state they live in. These hours are supervised by a seasoned licensed supervisor and are required to earn a license. These are broad categories and sometimes have variations. Plenty of biblical counselors go on to get their license. Many secularly trained therapists are believers and incorporate their faith into every aspect of their counseling practice. But these two categories generally represent the world of therapists you'll encounter in the twenty-first century.

Christians often wonder what type of counselor they should see. Should they go to a biblical counselor, a Christian licensed clinician, or one who isn't a believer at all? Christians have the freedom to choose any of these types of mental health professionals for help. Each of these types of counselors come with strengths and weaknesses. I've had clients see nonbelieving therapists for years for certain issues and found them to be helpful, yet they felt a disconnect related to overall worldview. Those same clients have then switched to me to have a therapist who will use biblical truth as part of their conversations. On the other hand, I've had clients see biblical counselors in their history and, again, found them to be helpful but felt some tools or recent research were missing in the journey toward health. The idea that only one or the other can be used by the Lord to care for you in your suffering is not a theologically accurate way to look at the world. The God of common grace isn't limited to helping you only through one type of person. As we've stated before, there are times you need different kinds of help to solve one big problem. (In the end, of course, and no matter what mix of helps a sufferer is receiving, we would be remiss not to recommend incorporating some sort of Christian influence in your healing process. To completely leave out a Christian influence in your journey—whether formal or informal—would be to miss out on the hope of the gospel and the Scriptures.)

Therapists are trained in different modalities or techniques used to counsel and help clients with anxiety. Remember that the biblical doctrine of common grace means that God uses all kinds of tools like seat belts, surgical instruments, and computer software to help push back against the fall and bring redemption. Counseling modalities are more of those tools. While many modalities are used to battle anxiety, we're going to name just a few and briefly describe them.

Cognitive behavioral therapy (**CBT**) focuses on changing negative thought patterns to change your feelings, leading to a change in behavior. The aim is that these changes will improve your mental health. CBT is effective with anxiety because much of our anxiety stems from our thoughts. CBT is 2 Corinthians 10:5 in therapy form: "We take every thought captive to obey Christ." With CBT, a therapist helps you change your thoughts to lead to changes in your behavior. If you're a believer, every step of this process must include an invitation to the Holy Spirit to enable this change to happen.

Eye movement desensitization and reprocessing (**EMDR**) can be an extremely helpful modality for treating anxiety whose root cause is trauma. Though the name is a mouthful, EMDR is a unique process that has proven to be effective.[2] The therapist has the client process a specific traumatic memory. While doing this, the therapist has the client engage in bilateral stimulation (activating both sides of the body and brain) with side-to-side eye movement, tapping, or auditory tones in a rhythmic way. The therapist guides the client through an eight-phase protocol that changes their relationship with the traumatic memory and its impact on their view of self. The idea here is that our traumatic memories can get stored the wrong way in our brains, not letting us move past them as we should. These intense memories get stuck in the brain, and our bodies need help reprocessing them, so they can get stored the right way. Brain spotting, another modality, also uses eye movement to help treat traumatic memories and lower anxiety. These can be game changers for someone struggling with anxiety and trauma.

Internal family systems (IFS) is another therapy commonly used to treat anxiety. I (Hope) often use this in my office. The idea behind it is that we aren't made up of just one part but several parts. Clients who use this type of therapy visualize their parts (for example, the "numbing" part of you, or the "people pleaser" part of you). Each of these parts is trying to do a "job" for you and "help" you but may not actually be helpful. Engaging with them in a compassionate way can change this. When I first introduce it, clients sometimes look at me like, "Are you crazy? Isn't this like multiple personality disorder?" I help them work through this thought by saying, "You know how sometimes we say, 'Part of me feels this way, and part of me feels that way?,'" in order to show them this is the natural way we talk about situations and problems. For many, it feels like a new or different way of interacting in the therapy room. However, people using IFS often report feeling like they can finally identify the narratives that have been bouncing around in their head that they were maybe aware of or unaware of. They also report that they are able to get some space from their anxiety and understand better how to engage with it.

Neurofeedback is a brain training tool that can help reduce anxiety. It uses a computer-based program to give immediate feedback about a client's brainwave activity. Using something interactive like a video game, the client learns how to change their brainwaves in real time. This can all be tailored to the type of anxiety the client is experiencing to help them reduce the anxiety-related brain activity. People often pair neurofeedback with counseling for effective treatment.

To reiterate what we've said before, none of these modalities should *replace* spiritual helps and habits in your Christian life. They are to be used *in tandem* with or as an *aid* to your walk with God. Think of it in terms of pain. When you have an intense headache, or arthritic pain, or a season of inflammation, of course you want to get up in the morning and glorify God and enjoy him in the life that he has placed you. But pain, and in this instance emotional pain, can be incredibly debilitating, making it difficult to show up in the places God has called you. There's a tool to help your body lower the pain level so you can continue to do what he has called you to do in this life: ibuprofen. These tools are not what we depend on to give us life, but God can use them to help us get back to the practices and spiritual disciplines that root us in Christ. Anxiety modalities are similar. They aren't the point; rather, they help you lessen the impact of the debilitating bodily responses you wake up to each morning so you can get to the point.

Medication

Medication can be extremely helpful in reducing anxiety and its effects, but it's the one tool that my Christian clients resist the most. Often, they will tell me they just need more faith, not medication. They believe medication is a crutch that keeps them from trusting God. I have heard this hundreds of times. This is just one more place where letting theology inform our insight about mental health is so important. If our brains fell in the garden along with our hearts, that means sometimes our brains aren't producing the chemicals they were intended to produce to help regulate us. As he's done throughout history, God has given us medical inventions to minimize the effects of the fall on the body. Antidepressants are one of those things. Some people use them just for a season, some for decades. They can greatly change a person's ability to function and engage in life. Sometimes taking medication isn't a lack of faith; it's a step of faith.

Understandably, some people may worry about side effects of medication like feeling numb, foggy, or out of touch with their feelings. They may fear these drugs will change their personality. If you've had any of these side effects, you may not be on the medication that is right for you. Psychiatrists can be helpful in giving evidence-based insight about specific concerns, guiding people to their best medication option in their specific situation. Medication has been proven effective in treating anxiety. But it may not be the right fit for you. Medication is just one of many options.

God created all kinds of natural treatments for anxiety as well. Some people may even find that these are more effective than medication. Lavender pills, rescue remedy products, magnesium, ashwagandha, 5-HTP, and GABA have all had positive results for some in treating their anxiety. While we are not medical providers and these things should be discussed with your doctor before taking them, all have been reported as helpful in my practice.

Not If It's Sin

While this wonderful array of treatments is available for believers in their fight against anxiety, some things are not permitted—anything that leads to sin. This may seem obvious when outside the process, but it needs to be said. We cannot justify sinful practices as a means to an end of relieving anxiety (or depression). For example, the relationship between a therapist and his or her client is an intimate and vulnerable one. A client and therapist can decide to have an emotional and/or physical affair that feels good and may temporarily decrease the client's anxiety. However, the relief brought doesn't justify the sin of the affair. The same could be said for abuse of alcohol or other substances, gossiping about friends to make yourself feel better about your own circumstances, or stealing money from work to decrease anxiety about your personal finances. Any practice that is sinful or leads to sin should be avoided by God's people.

Working with Our Design

We will discuss life rhythms that benefit mental wellness overall in chapter 8, but for now let's focus on specific, practical tools for your anxiety. The reason these tools work is because they work with our design as humans and not against it. Psalm 103:14 reads, "For he knows what we are made of, remembering that we are dust." He knows how we are put together, what parts of his design are prone to be triggered by anxiety and what parts can help calm them down.

As we mentioned in chapter 3, the brain and nervous system often react to both depression and anxiety. When someone has a huge surge of anxiety, it hijacks both their body and their mind. This is why we get that panicked feeling—fight, flight, freeze, or fawn—and have all kinds of body sensations like a racing heart, a tight chest, and shortness of breath, among other things. The following tools help calm the brain and activate the parasympathetic nervous system to help us lower anxiety and increase calmness.

Breathing

One often overlooked but immediately available tool that can help you when heightened is breathing. Pay attention next time you get anxious. You might notice that you almost start to hold your breath. This is the opposite of what your body needs at this moment. Taking deep breaths when anxious immediately sends a signal to activate the destressing part of your nervous system. Fearfully and wonderfully made. Am I right? You can do this anytime, anywhere. Want to learn more? Look up "box breathing" to give yourself a ready technique in your next moment of panic.

Moving Your Body

Moving your body, like breathing, can have an almost immediate impact on anxiety. A short walk, a quick dance, or a set of jumping jacks releases all kinds of feel-good chemicals that help your brain move you into a positive mood. Next time you're anxious, take a quick walk around your block or turn on a fun song and dance around your kitchen. You might be surprised by the little lift this naturally gives to your brain.[3]

Staying in the Present

Anxiety is an expert at dragging people out of the present into the future. And not just any future but a future filled with the worst-case scenario possible. We often use our minds to build terrible ideas of what the future will look like and then play them like movies in our mind, dragging our nervous system and emotions through the whole thing. I (Hope) once had a wise woman say to me that God doesn't live in our fake, worst-case scenarios of the future; he lives with us in the present. He promises to be with us today in what is real. Not in a place that is *not* real and only in our heads. Just doing the next five minutes or staying on today's tasks or problems helps slow our anxiety down. Jesus said in Matthew 6:34, "Therefore don't worry about tomorrow, because tomorrow will worry about itself. Each day has enough trouble of its own." Jesus is calling us to stay in the present.

Stop Stacking

Anxious people tend to take a bunch of things that feel overwhelming and flood themselves by thinking about them all at once. This can be a to-do list or a series of circumstances. Imagine you have a stack of bricks on top of a table. Each brick represents something that's giving you anxiety. Imagine lying down and stacking those bricks one on top of the other on your chest until they reach the ceiling. This is what anxious people do in their minds with their thoughts. Instead, what if you took the bricks and put them side by side on the table? You could leave space in between them and touch them one at a time. Give them the space and attention they need instead of piling them up.

How might you do this? First, get out a piece of paper and write down all of the "bricks," the things that feel stressful to you at one time. Then, assign specific "bricks" to specific times on your calendar to give yourself time to think through or do them, depending on what they are. That way you aren't trying to flood your anxious brain with so many "assignments," making it more anxious and unable to problem solve in a way that's helpful. I know you might be thinking, *That sounds impossible!* But if you find your mind wandering, tell yourself, "That's not the task or the thing I need to be working on or thinking about right now. That's for my future self to do tomorrow or next week or next year. For now, I'm going to set that brick aside for later and focus on the brick in front of me." This concept helps the anxious brain stay in the present.

Spiritual Tools and Rhythms

Scripture Meditation

Paul wrote to his beloved church in Philippi: "Don't worry about anything, but in everything, through prayer and petition with thanksgiving, present your requests to God. And the peace of God, which surpasses all understanding, will guard your hearts and minds in Christ Jesus" (Phil. 4:6–7). Paul was offering prayer as an alternative to worry, but he also gave a promise that every anxious person needs: peace. This is not any peace but the peace of God, which is able to guard hearts and minds, even anxious ones. One way toward this peace is to replace the racing thoughts of anxiety with the solid, trustworthy words of God through Scripture meditation.

Don't be discouraged if your first few attempts to meditate are wildly unsuccessful. Your mind has been trained by anxiety to think about everything *but* Scripture. Meditation is a discipline that takes time and practice, and there are many resources to help you learn to do it well. There is true wealth to be gained by this training of your mind if you will commit to it. Just as you might begin weight training by committing a couple of hours every week to strengthen your body, so you might train your mind by committing a few minutes a day to populate your mind with God's good promises. Here are just a few examples of the treasure trove of Scripture for the anxious mind:

- Hebrews 13:6 (ESV): "So we can confidently say, 'The Lord is my helper; I will not fear; what can man do to me?'"
- Psalm 23 (ESV): "The LORD is my shepherd; I shall not want. He makes me lie down in green pastures. He leads me beside still waters. He restores my soul. He leads me in paths of righteousness for his name's sake. Even though I walk through the valley of the shadow of death, I will fear no evil, for you are with me; your rod and your staff, they comfort me. You prepare a table before me in the presence of my enemies; you anoint my head with oil; my cup overflows. Surely goodness and mercy shall follow me all the days of my life, and I shall dwell in the house of the LORD forever."
- Proverbs 3:5–6 (ESV): "Trust in the LORD with all your heart, and do not lean on your own understanding. In all your ways acknowledge him, and he will make straight your paths."
- Isaiah 26:3 (NIV): "You will keep in perfect peace those whose minds are steadfast, because they trust in you."
- Isaiah 41:10 (ESV): "Fear not, for I am with you; be not dismayed, for I am your God; I will strengthen you, I will help you, I will uphold you with my righteous right hand."
- Romans 8:28 (NIV): "And we know that in all things God works for the good of those who love him, who have been called according to his purpose."
- Matthew 11:28 (NIV): "Come to me, all you who are weary and burdened, and I will give you rest."

- Isaiah 43:1–4 (ESV): "Fear not, for I have redeemed you; I have called you by name, you are mine. When you pass through the waters, I will be with you; and through the rivers, they shall not overwhelm you; when you walk through fire you shall not be burned, and the flame shall not consume you. For I am the LORD your God, the Holy One of Israel, your Savior. . . . You are precious in my eyes, and honored, and I love you."

Remember as you meditate on God's Word that the Word himself is with you. You are not in this fight alone. The one who created you still holds you together and gives you every breath and heartbeat. As Paul writes in Colossians 1:17, "He is before all things, and by him all things hold together." Call on the Holy Spirit to help you as you depend on him in this struggle.

Worship

Worship can feel like the last thing you want to do when struggling with anxiety. Why would you sing praise to God or repeat his beautiful attributes when your mind is spinning with fear and dread of what might be coming? Worship grounds you and can be a pathway out of your anxiety. Worship is not a denial of the trouble you feel you're facing or a choice to ignore whatever real responsibility you have to act. Worship is a reorientation to what's true. It's reminding yourself of who's in charge of the world and your relationship to him.

Worshipping God when you're anxious is like using the horizon indicator in a plane in a thick fog. If you can't see where the land meets the sky through your windows because of the clouds all around you, the horizon indicator is the tool that will always orient you to that line. Worship works like that in your heart. When anxiety feels so thick that you cannot orient yourself in the world, worship will remind you that God is powerful, good, and loving, and that you can trust him. So create a playlist with all your favorite worship songs, and surround yourself with praise whenever you can—in the car, while you're doing chores in the house, or in the background as you answer emails. However you can fit it in, prioritize worship and let it help you do exactly as it helped the psalmist do: "Bless the LORD, O my soul, and forget not all his benefits" (Ps. 103:2 ESV).

The Power of Community

All believers know that we're called to live in community with others, to confess sin, share our burdens, worship together, and celebrate our joys with those around us. For believers who struggle with anxiety, community can have huge benefits. While I realize community can also make us anxious, a healthy community can be a grounding presence and help anxious sisters and brothers get off the hamster wheel in their mind. Sharing with others the intrusive thoughts that are keeping you up at night or pounding on you all day long is a powerful tool in co-regulation. *Regulation* is a fancy clinical word that means "bringing your body back to a state of calm." When we co-regulate, meaning with others and not by ourselves, we calm down exponentially faster than we do alone.

I (Hope) was recently on a cramped tram in an airport. A mom stepped on with a tiny baby strapped to her chest. He was crying, and I could tell that she was about to start as well. I placed my hand on her shoulder and made eye contact, and she started crying. I said, "I know this is so hard. You're doing so well, big deep breaths." She took several breaths and started to calm down. At that moment I helped her co-regulate. We also can co-regulate with God through prayer—his steady presence there in the moment as our *Paraclete* (the helper and friend who "comes alongside" us in John 14:16), helping us calm down. Pretty amazing!

Holy Imagination

So often when we begin to feel anxious, we feed our anxiety by filling our minds with terrible images of horrible things happening, adding faces and details to our fears so that they feel real and certain. Neuroscience tells us that when we do this over and over, we form well-traveled highways of fear that our minds easily return to over and over. But our minds are capable of imagining good as well as evil. Our brains can form new pathways, new ways of thinking, because of an amazing ability called "neuroplasticity." We can literally change our brain's structure. It will be hard work at first, like hacking out a jungle path with a machete. But as you do it over and over, it will get easier each time, until it replaces the highway you used to use.

As believers we can employ a "holy imagination," using our minds to imagine how God might intervene in our current situation. We can make a new neural path by visualizing God providing the money we need, protecting our husband as he travels, or encouraging one of our children through a teacher or friend. To be clear, visualizations like this don't put God on the hook for granting a situational result that aligns exactly with our every hope or dream. Rather, the practice of envisioning God as good, involved, and provisional helps us recall (and trust in!) his character as our good Father and replaces our habit of catastrophizing.

Prayer

The Psalms are filled with expressions of anxiety and requests for God's help in the midst of it. Psalm 61:1–4 reads: "God, hear my cry; pay attention to my prayer. I call to you from the ends of the earth when my heart is without strength. Lead me to a rock that is high above me, for you have been a refuge for me, a strong tower in the face of the enemy. I will dwell in your tent forever and take refuge under the shelter of your wings."

David calls out to God when his "heart is without strength." He's feeling vulnerable, needy, and desperate—three basic building blocks of anxiety. He asks for a safe place where he is protected even when his enemies come near. He soothes himself with thoughts of God sheltering him like a mother bird shelters her babies with her wings from all kinds of weather and predators. David's words are a wonderful template for our prayers when we are feeling anxious. We can pray his words or craft our own similar prayers.

We find more to pray in the Psalms, including words that express and give comfort for the heart when holding specific anxieties. Psalm 27:9–10 shows and then soothes a fear of abandonment: "Do not hide your face from me; do not turn your servant away in anger. You have been my helper; do not leave me or abandon me, God of my salvation. Even if my father and mother abandon me, the LORD cares for me."

The Lord was kind to his people when he inspired the words of many psalms to articulate different anxieties. He knew you would need help voicing your fear and laying your worries at his feet. He gave you a songbook to sing your fear to him. Your prayers don't have to be well articulated or even make sense in moments of anxiety. A simple cry of "help" is heard by your God. Peter reminds you that you should speak to God, "casting all your cares on him, because he cares about you" (1 Pet. 5:7).

Remembering

Maybe you've attended some kind of testimony time in a campus ministry or a church. It's encouraging to hear stories about God answering secret prayers, providing in desperate situations, and meeting people in their pain. You're reminded of how God's nearness and care looks in the everyday lives of people you know. The stories you hear reinforce for your heart what your mind already knows: God hears, God sees, God cares.

The psalmist is our example as he writes in Psalm 77:11–14: "I will remember the LORD's works; yes, I will remember your ancient wonders. I will reflect on all you have done and meditate on your actions. God, your way is holy. What god is great like God? You are the God who works wonders; you revealed your strength among the peoples."

You don't have to wait for a church service to experience the boost to your faith given by testimonies. Think back on your own life or even just the last few months. Where have you seen God act? When has he provided what or whom you needed? Think through a specific story or two and the specificity of God's care. Maybe even tell someone else one of your stories. Let his work in your own life remind you of who he is and how he has met you in the past. Let your history with God inform your future. Expect him to be the same faithful God today that he has been before. Hear the words of Psalm 105:5 encouraging you: "Remember the wondrous works he has done, his wonders, and the judgments he has pronounced."

Over the last twenty-five years I (Hope) have had four major, debilitating bouts of anxiety, not to mention the low-grade presence of it daily. But I'm also able to trace Jesus's nearness to me and deep care in this place of desperation and suffering. Nothing quiets me like remembering how he always shows up in this area of my life. He turns something that once was so terrifying into a place of connection between me and him. And for you, dear one, struggling so deeply: I know he sees you, too, even if that feels hard to believe in the worst moments. In your panic and waves of fear, reach out and co-regulate with your Father who loves you.

Questions for Reflection

1. What from Hope's story of anxiety can you relate to?

2. What surprised you or was a new way of thinking regarding what tools are okay for you to use as a believer in combating anxiety?

3. Which of the practical tools would you like to try? Which of the spiritual tools would you like to try?

4. A combination of tools is needed in order to have a holistic approach to anxiety. What tools do you think would be the most helpful in your "pie"?

Chapter 7
Dealing with Your Depression

"When I sit in darkness, the Lord will be a light to me."
Micah 7:8 ESV

Part of the Lord's completing a good work in you includes his work against the effects of the fall in all areas of your life. God gives you ways to treat things like depression and experience some measure of relief. Sometimes this help comes through new ways of thinking. Sometimes it comes through new ways of functioning. Sometimes God eliminates the struggle altogether.

Christine's Depression Story

The counselor across from me (Christine) presented a question: "Do you mind if I record this session? The only person who will listen to it is my supervisor, and it's to help train me as I work toward my license."

Well, this session's gonna be a doozy, lady, I thought to myself as I gave my yes answer. It was only the third time I'd seen Laura, but she seemed like she actually cared about what I was saying. Her habitual Diet Cokes during sessions along with her bag stuffed under her desk somehow made me more comfortable. She was human; I figured she probably drank Diet Coke to help her stay awake as people on her couch talked on and on.

"So I took a bunch of pills this weekend when my roommates were gone," I began. Her face betrayed a little bit of shock, but she remained calm. This was one of the things I eventually loved about counselors, their experience with people like me. I wasn't the first to tell Laura something like this, and I wouldn't be the last. The session ended with her asking me to sign a contract promising that I wouldn't try to hurt myself before the next time we met. It seemed a silly thing, a strange "contract" to sign with this woman I barely knew. But I thought about that contract numerous times in the week that followed.

What Tools Are Okay to Use?

Years later I (Christine) found myself working as an intake coordinator for a large counseling practice. All the therapists on staff were believers, so the practice attracted many Christians seeking help. While people sought treatment for all types of mental illness, depression was a frequent instigator of phone calls to my intake phone. I heard stories of unexpected and tragic loss that left survivors struggling to cope with their pain. I heard about slow, steady slides down the spiral of sadness into a depression that lingered for months. Some had eagerly anticipated the birth of a child and then were confused by their postpartum depression that made it difficult to enjoy their baby. Others felt fine until the darker months of winter seemed to suck away all their energy.

In the mix of hundreds of questions and stories, I heard fear and uncertainty about what treatment might be like. "Yes, but is she a *Christian* therapist, really?" "So, will this counselor try to convince my daughter she needs to take medication? Because I don't think Christians should do that." "My faith is important to me. Can that be a part of my therapy?" "Do your counselors use *secular* treatments?" "What if I'm not a Christian? Can I still be seen?"

Maybe you're in a similar place with similar questions as you seek help for depression. What's a believer to do? What tools are available and appropriate for us to use in our fight against depression? As already stated in the previous chapter on anxiety, here comes some good news: There are so many! Again, remember from chapter 4 that all truth is God's truth. All true things we discover in the world, whether they are the rules of thermodynamics or the way our neurotransmitters work, are truths that belong to God about things created by God. Unless a method or treatment causes us to sin, we can use the wide array of tools offered in this world to push back against the effects of the fall and specifically the effect of depression.

As you read the sections below, note that the tools listed there are not in any particular order suggesting effectiveness or preference. We'd like to end the chapter with the hope and spiritual power that God's Word and God's people offer us. Also, recall from chapter 6 that Jesus is the Great Physician. He holds us and attends us as we suffer. Ask him to help you and to empower the change you're seeking because there's no changing or healing without Christ!

Therapy

Therapy can be an incredibly helpful tool when it comes to treating depression. It gives the sufferer a place to get all the sad thoughts out of their head and into the hands of someone who can help sort them out. The therapist can also help establish rhythms to lessen the weight of the depression and help the sufferer notice tiny rays of joy peeking through. In the instances where the client has thoughts of suicide, the therapist can provide life-saving guidance and emergency help. And more good news: Therapies like EMDR, CBT, and IFS that are helpful with anxiety can also be helpful with depression. The therapist simply adjusts these tools accordingly.

Transcranial magnetic stimulation (TMS) is a highly effective treatment for depression, though people often look at you sideways when you explain it. For TMS treatment you sit in a chair with a machine stationed above your head that sends short, magnetic pulses to the limbic system of the brain to stimulate nerve cells. This stimulation improves symptoms of depression and sometimes sends people's depression completely into remission. It may be slightly irritating at first to the scalp, but these symptoms almost always resolve by the middle of treatment. This treatment has proved to be highly effective![1] I (Christine) have used this treatment and found it to be helpful.

Electroconvulsive therapy (**ECT**) can greatly reduce the effects of major depressive disorder and is often used when all other options have been exhausted. What the actual treatment entails can feel startling to people. Using electric impulses, a doctor induces a seizure in the patient's brain while they are under anesthesia. They do this a set number of times over a series of weeks for the treatment to have its full effect. Some people who have been beaten and battered by depression for years have credited this treatment with saving their lives.[2]

Many other types of treatment exist to push against the effects of depression, such as vagus nerve stimulation and ketamine. These, along with other lesser-known treatments, can be a huge help to the weary struggler.[3]

Medication

As we mentioned in chapter 6, the resistance people feel about taking medication for depression can be strong. Depressed Christians tend to give the same reasons for refusing medication that anxious ones do. They hesitate because they see medication as a crutch or evidence of a weak faith. Some worry about being on medication for any reason because of possible side effects. All of this makes sense. Research has shown time and time again that meds can be a game changer when it comes to treating depression.[4] Medications can help minimize the effects of the fall on the brain systems that process emotions. Sometimes it can take trying a few different medications to find the one or ones that work.

If medication feels too intimidating or you've tried it and the side effects have outweighed the benefits, taking a natural supplement might feel like a better fit. Again, we are not medical professionals, and it is so important to discuss use of any supplements with yours.

Natural options that have been shown to be helpful are saffron,[5] SAMe, and lavender pills as well as others.

While these many treatments and medications are available for believers in their fight against depression, anything that leads to sin is *not* permitted. As mentioned in the treatment of anxiety, this needs to be said, though it may seem obvious to those outside the struggle. We cannot justify sinful practices as a means to an end of relieving depression.

Working with Our Design

Energy

Depression is notorious for making people feel sluggish and sleepy. You may have trouble concentrating or even getting yourself to do daily activities like take a shower or get dressed. Your nervous system needs a reset, a restart. "Upregulating" is a technique that can help with this needed restart. Exercise, listening to energizing music, or anything that gets your blood pumping is a great way to upregulate your system. What things do you do in life that afterward you think, *Wow, I feel better after that!* Maybe it's spending time with friends, watching a comedian who makes you laugh really hard, going on a walk, or cleaning out a messy drawer. Figure out what specific things reenergize you, and ask a friend to help make sure you do them.

Sunlamps

For people who struggle with depression, living in a place that has long, dark winters can make them more prone to a struggle with seasonal affective disorder (SAD). Sunlamps mimic natural sunlight and can be highly effective in helping battle SAD. Why is this? Because this bright light tells the brain to release serotonin, a mood booster, and helps regulate our sleep rhythms. I (Christine) have used a sunlamp every fall through spring for many years and have found it helpful in fighting seasonal affective disorder.[6]

Body/Emotion Awareness

Sometimes when people struggle with depression, sadness is such a strong, overarching emotion that it's hard for them to recognize when they feel other things. Often, they can't identify anything *but* the sadness. The truth is, even when we do feel sad, even clinically depressed, other emotions peek through. It's important to notice them to help turn down the sadness a bit. One way to do this includes basic body and emotion awareness. Often the first place we feel emotions is in our bodies. Reading your body can help you figure out what you're feeling.

- Does my body feel relaxed? I'm feeling peace.
- Are my shoulders and chest tight? I'm feeling fear.
- Do I feel an excitement in my stomach and a pep in my step? I'm feeling joy.
- Do I feel a heavy, deep ache? I'm feeling sad.

Another helpful tool for discerning emotions is a feelings wheel. You can easily purchase one online. These wheels give a variety of words to choose from to see that sadness is not all you're experiencing. Sometimes just naming these other emotions can help you feel less overtaken by depression.

Recognizing and Stopping the Spiral

Much like anxiety, depression has its own cycle of thoughts that can drag a person down. While anxiety thoughts can drag you into a panic attack, depressive thoughts can drag you into a sad spiral that can lead to debilitating despair. Because this can become second nature to a depressed person, you may not even recognize that you've begun jumping from sad thought to sad thought until you've painted your whole world and future a deep shade of despair. Even realizing that you're doing this gives you the opportunity to interrupt these thoughts and inject other thoughts into the mix. Prayer and Scripture can serve as wonderful interrupters of a sad spiral, as they help you remember that God speaks a better word over you than spiraling thoughts do!

Movement

Recall from chapter 2 that exercise releases endorphins, which produce euphoria and improve your mood overall. In my (Christine's) more than thirty-five-year fight with depression, I have yet to find a treatment that produces results as immediate as exercise. Any type of movement can help: brisk walks, yard work, pickup basketball games, or weight lifting. Anything that raises your heart rate can help combat depression. Figure out what you enjoy doing and maybe ask a friend to do it with you.

Sleep and Fuel

Remember Elijah's story from 1 Kings 19? Elijah had come from a high in ministry but then experienced a very low low. His depression brought him to a place where he sat down under a tree and asked God to take his life. Notice what God did. As Elijah's Creator and his good Father, God knew what Elijah needed at that moment. He didn't need a pep talk, a rebuke for his lack of faith, or a call to action. Elijah needed food and rest. He had traveled multiple days on foot without nourishment. He was exhausted and depleted. God sent an angel to attend him, food to sustain him, and sleep to revive him. After that, God provided more help in other forms to Elijah, but he began by tending to Elijah's physical needs for food and sleep.

Sleep is foundational for mental health. One of the first things you can do as you explore all the tools possible to help improve your anxiety or depression is to evaluate your sleep schedule. There are many resources to help you improve your sleep, but the biggest help may be just a reminder that it's important! I (Christine) know that when my sleep isn't regular or is too little, I struggle to regulate in any situation. Be careful with the other direction as well. *Too much* sleep can make you sluggish and also affect your mood. One of my first indicators of a bout of depression coming on is usually that I want to sleep more than usual.

Fuel is just behind sleep in its importance. Your gut has been named the "second brain" and has a part to play in neurotransmitter production, influencing mood and energy levels. It may feel like a real drag to go for the vegetables instead of the nachos, but long-term nutrition can have an impact on long-term mood.

Spiritual Tools and Rhythms

Prayer and Worship

Do you ever wonder why the psalmists talk so much to their own souls? Consider the first few verses of Psalm 103 (ESV): "Bless the LORD, O my soul, and all that is within me, bless his holy name! Bless the LORD, O my soul, and forget not all his benefits, who forgives all your iniquity, who heals all your diseases, who redeems your life from the pit, who crowns you with steadfast love and mercy, who satisfies you with good so that your youth is renewed like the eagle's" (vv. 1–5).

Or Psalm 42:5 (ESV): "Why are you cast down, O my soul, and why are you in turmoil within me? Hope in God; for I shall again praise him, my salvation."

Or Psalm 116:7 (ESV): "Return, O my soul, to your rest; for the LORD has dealt bountifully with you."

The psalmists were like us and sometimes had souls that needed to be reminded of God's love and work for them. These psalms and others can be used as templates for us as we speak to our own souls, reminding them that the voices we often hear are lying to us. Whether it's a critical mother, a cruel or absent father, or a thoughtless wife or husband who left a recording in your mind of painful words, these psalms and other truths of Scripture can help you fight back and think on the truth instead.

God does not need our worship, but we certainly need to worship him! Worship takes our eyes off the passing suffering of this present life and returns our eyes to the one who never struggles or sleeps. He is always beautiful, majestic, and in control. We need a true vision of God to fill our eyes and hearts instead of our own pain, which can feel like it's going to fill up all our thoughts.

Worship can be difficult in the midst of depression. Try anyway. Put on your favorite worship music and ask God to pull you up by his Spirit. Go to church and actually sing. Do it before you slide down the spiral, at the first sight of depressed symptoms. Satan wants you to panic and believe there is nothing you can do to get out of depression's grip. Fight back with worship and prayer. And probably most importantly, ask others to pray for you. Though depression can obviously be a physiological problem, it can also be spiritual. We don't always know which it is so it's best to worship either way!

Community

Community makes such a difference in walking through life, and walking through depression is no different. Consider Hope's perspective here: When Christine and I (Hope) lived in the same town, Christine's depression would usually take a turn for the worst in the winter months. That time of year it was cold, dark, and sometimes icy outside. I remember Christine asking me to walk with her early in the morning, before kids were up, to help her battle her depression. Because it was so cold outside and ridiculously early, we went to the local grocery store and walked laps inside. During that season we also went sledding together so she wouldn't be home alone with her kids and her thoughts on a rare snow day. These gestures—just getting out of the house together to move our bodies and let in some light—may seem small. But to someone who struggles with depression, they can be the lifeline that gets them through that day.

Lament

God provided a fabulous tool for all believers that is often unused: lament. Lament is a complaint to God. It's a prayer in pain that leads to trust.[7] Lament involves pouring out your heart to the

Lord, telling him about loss, suffering, destruction, and injustice. It requires brutal honesty about the difficulties and disappointments in your life.

The idea of lament can make Christians uncomfortable because of messages they've heard from their families or models of prayer they've seen. Many of us have been told we can never say anything negative or complaint-like to God as it would be disrespectful or show our lack of faith. Verses like, "Do everything without grumbling and arguing" (Phil. 2:14) are used to remind believers of what they are and aren't allowed to say. But complaining to God is different from complaining to others. God actually invites complaint when it's directed *to* him instead of away from him. Said another way, grumbling is gossiping about God behind his back, whether by thoughts that live in your own head or in conversations with others. Lament is bringing painful grievances directly to God, which he welcomes.

The Psalms are full of individual and corporate laments, offering templates for pouring your heart out to God. The book of Lamentations records five chapters of lament as the city of Jerusalem was destroyed by God's enemies. Instead of stuffing your pain when you talk to God, your Father invites you to bring all of it to him, that you might learn to trust him even with the worst parts of life and stay connected to him in the middle of them. Psalms 13; 77; and 130 are great places to begin learning to lament.

Scripture Meditation

The Bible also gives us plenty of verses to help us see pinpricks of light in our darkness. Hope is always present because God is present. But we may need to push ourselves to look for it. Consider a few examples of light and hope found throughout the Scriptures:

> Psalm 139:11–12: "If I say, 'Surely the darkness will hide me, and the light around me will be night'—even the darkness is not dark to you. The night shines like the day; darkness and light are alike to you."

Psalm 62:5: "Rest in God alone, my soul, for my hope comes from him."

Psalm 39:7: "Now, Lord, what do I wait for? My hope is in you."

Psalm 71:5: "For you are my hope, Lord God, my confidence from my youth."

1 John 1:5: "This is the message we have heard from him and declare to you: God is light, and there is absolutely no darkness in him."

Ephesians 5:8: "For you were once darkness, but now you are light in the Lord."

Suicidal Thoughts

I (Christine) have had particularly hard weeks and months where suicide was like an escape route I always had in mind in case of emergency. I always wanted the option available and would fantasize about leaving this world on really bad days. These terribly dark thoughts are referred to by clinicians as suicidal ideation (SI). They can be repetitive and intrusive. They pound on a depressed person regularly, sometimes daily. People who experience these thoughts often feel overwhelmed with pain and want to escape. Sometimes they believe the world would be better without them in it. The tools we've mentioned can greatly help decrease these thoughts. If you struggle in this way, save the suicide hotline in your phone for emergencies (988). Even more importantly, make your loved ones and mental health providers aware of your SI. Also remember that you can go to a local ER at any hour if you feel like you're a danger to yourself. There you will be assessed and kept safe. Bringing thoughts of suicide out into the light can cut down on the shame that our enemy (Satan) wants to heap on you while you silently struggle. Just having a conversation can also lower the intensity of these thoughts.

One way to think about these thoughts and assess their level of intensity is to think of them as flying birds. If you have a suicidal thought "fly" over your head, that's one thing. If that "bird" stops and lands on your head, that's more serious. And if it builds a "nest" in your thoughts where it takes up residence, that's even more serious. This can help you and your loved ones determine what intervention is needed, again showing how necessary it is to have others involved.

Over the years some of my (Hope) clients who love Jesus and chronically struggle with suicidal ideation have learned that this is part of the suffering they will bear in this life. These urges can come and go for some individuals. It is a remarkable show of faith when a believer suffers in this way and still seeks after Jesus.

Depression can be a heavy, relentless form of suffering in this broken world. But we've not been left to struggle without help. Believe it or not, those who love you really do want to know about your depression. Your struggle is not a reason for shame. Jesus is not ashamed of you (Heb. 2:11). And he has given you the good gifts of therapy, medication, community, Scripture, prayer, and many other tools to help you. If you struggle, don't give into the dark thoughts that threaten to pull you down into despair. Reach out to those who love you, to your clinicians, and most often, to your Maker. He is never far from you. "The LORD is near the brokenhearted; he saves those crushed in spirit" (Ps. 34:18).

Questions for Reflection

1. What about Christine's story of depression resonated with you?

2. What surprised you or was a new way of thinking regarding what tools are okay for you to use as a believer in combating depression?

3. Which of the practical tools would you like to try? Which of the spiritual tools would you like to try?

4. A combination of tools is needed to have a holistic approach to depression. What tools do you think would be the most helpful?

Chapter 8

Faithful Stewardship

"We know that all things work together for the good of those who love God, who are called according to his purpose. For those he foreknew he also predestined to be conformed to the image of his Son, so that he would be the firstborn among many brothers and sisters."

Romans 8:28–29

I (Christine) was twenty-five-years old the first time a counselor named "depression" for me. I was in seminary full time and was always working at least two jobs. Between learning Greek verbs and teaching ESL, there hadn't been much margin to get help. But this lovely woman gave me categories. Not only did she direct me to a psychiatrist for possible medication, but she also asked me questions about my body: How much was I sleeping? Did I ever take a day off? Was I getting enough calories? It took months, but I started to see that there were specific things I could do that helped. It surprised me that habits with my *body* actually affected my *mood* and outlook. I started to learn how to steward my body instead of being controlled by it.

But does stewardship start with me? Am I in charge of all of this for myself? What is stewardship anyway? Like most things in our life with God, in his goodness, he is the instigator, the first mover, the one who begins the good work. Not only will he start it; he'll finish it. Philippians 1:6 reads, "I am sure of this, that he who started a good work in you will carry it on to completion until the day of Christ Jesus." He's committed to making us like Jesus, and the work will only be done when we see him face-to-face. He says something similar in 1 Thessalonians 5:23–24, "Now may the God of peace himself sanctify you completely. And may your whole spirit, soul, and body be kept sound and blameless at the coming of our Lord Jesus Christ. He who calls you is faithful; he will do it."

Stewardship is caring well for the resources God has given us. We steward what God has given us, but God also stewards *us*. Paul wrote about this in Ephesians 1:9–10: "[God] made known to us the mystery of His will, according to His good pleasure that He planned in Him for the administration of the days of fulfillment—to bring everything together in the Messiah, both things in heaven and things on earth in Him" (HCSB). The Greek word οἰκονομίαν, translated as "administration" in the HCSB (and also in other translations[1]), refers to the management or stewardship of a household. It has to do with overseeing, administrating, and stewarding a plan. God manages and oversees the entire world, of course, but he does this with special concern regarding his own household, the church. He is overseeing Christ's body, working all things together for our good and bringing us safely into the fulfillment of all he has planned. He is managing the growth of his kingdom, guiding its citizens both collectively and individually until the day it is fully established on earth. He is handling the process of reconciling people (and the world) to himself through his Son and then guiding those people into glory. In short, as we said before, God is stewarding *us*.

In his wisdom, God uses all things as he manages our lives—hard and easy, good and bad. All our experiences, ups and downs in relationships, successes and failures. Even the malfunctions and failures of our bodies are used for our good and growth in this process. As James writes, "Consider it a great joy, my brothers and sisters, whenever you experience various trials, because you know that the testing of your faith produces endurance. And let endurance have its full effect, so that you may be mature and complete, lacking nothing" (James 1:2–4). Or consider how Paul puts it in Romans 8:28–29: "We know that all things work together for the good of those who love God, who are called according to his purpose. For those he foreknew he also predestined to be conformed to the image of his Son." As God slowly forms us into the mature and complete character of Christ, he even uses our anxiety and depression to do so. Does this surprise you?

Sanctification

This process of becoming more like Jesus over a lifetime is often referred to as "sanctification," and it's a part of life for every believer. In sanctification we learn to love God more and love our sin less. As one theologian wrote, "When I speak of a man growing in grace, I mean simply this—that his sense of sin is becoming deeper, his faith stronger, his hope brighter, his love more extensive, his spiritual-mindedness more marked."[2] This is not a smooth step-by-step process, though many of us wish it was! In our life of obedience, we often take one step forward and two steps back, walk in a circle for a bit, and then take a short break. We try to love Jesus, fail, repent, try again, and learn more of his grace while we do so. But we're never on our own in this process. It's always God working first, and then we respond. As Paul wrote in Philippians 2:12–13, "Therefore, my dear friends, just as you have always obeyed, so now, not only in my presence but even more in my absence, work out your own salvation with fear and trembling. For it is God who is working in you both to will and to work according to his good purpose." We work out our salvation, learning to live faithfully before a holy God, but always because he's at work in us. God works so we work.

What does sanctification look like practically over time? People often look for big changes to show them sanctification is happening, while it usually happens through small changes. Think millimeters and centimeters of growth—not always feet and yards. You will also see this sanctifying work change your view of progress regarding anxiety and depression over the course of your lifetime. For me (Hope), I have seen it in a million little places. It's easier for me to get on planes. When a panic sensation starts in my body, it doesn't take over; I know how to navigate it. When I'm stuck in a rumination cycle, I can find my way off the hamster wheel faster. Yes, I still live with anxiety. But through his work of sanctification, God has helped me understand him and myself so much more, lessening the impact of anxiety on my daily life. By God's mercy and help, I can sense the small steps of growth over time.

For me (Christine), the world has gotten brighter over the past thirty years. I don't only notice all the sad things. I also see the beauty, feel the joyful moments, and look forward to good things. I have learned to celebrate, to savor good moments without letting the inevitable sadness take them over and encourage others to hope. I can ask for help more quickly when I feel the spiral of darkness starting to suck me down. I have learned ways to fight despair. I may always struggle with depression, but God has enabled me to function and even thrive during sad things. Like Hope, I too can sense the small steps of progress as God guides my journey with depression.

What Does God's Stewardship Mean for Us?

Because God is in charge of our spiritual formation and our Christlike transformation, and because he has guaranteed the process, we can live with a certain hope and freedom no matter our circumstances. If God has the power to use *all things* in our sanctification, it means we don't need to panic at every place of struggle or area where we suffer. God has the administrative authority and transformative power to use all of those things to make us more like Christ. Let's look at some of those things he uses and how we might therefore steward our own bodies in the process.

Gift of Limits

Every human life comes with limits, no matter how healthy or good. We can only stay awake so long, carry so much, and think about so many things. We must take breaks, sleep about one-third of our lives, and care for our bodies. We depend on God to provide food and protection, love and nurture. We depend on other people for companionship and help. None of these things are the result of sin; all of these limits were in place before Adam and Eve ate the fruit in the garden. God made us limited humans on purpose, dependent on him and other people. Stop and think about that thought for a second.

After sin entered the world, lots of other limits entered with it. Disease or disability may limit our ability to walk, care for children, work, or think clearly for a short or long period. We may lose a job and face strict limits as we try to make ends meet while we look for another. Loss of relationships because someone moves away or dies may mean our ability to think clearly or work efficiently is limited. Anxiety and depression may limit our ability to relate well to others, work productively, or function well in our everyday lives.

How is any of the above good news for our sanctification? Why would anyone call these limits a gift? In the wisdom of Christ's upside-down kingdom, he uses all these limits to help us know him better and in the process to be changed into his likeness. Living with anxiety for so long has forced me (Hope) to learn how to pray. It's taught me how to find Jesus in moments of fear. It's helped me see the progression of sanctification in my life. I know what anxiety used to feel like in certain situations in my life, and I know what that anxiety feels like today. Those moments are different, changed, better, easier to handle. Jesus has worked through my anxiety and has taught me to trust him, which is always a net good. Over the years I have learned how faithful he is and how to move through those anxious moments. I am calmer, less triggered, less stuck in my head. This is part of what sanctification looks like and how God uses anxiety to change me.

Your most difficult limit may come in the form of a "thorn" like the one Paul talks about in 2 Corinthians 12:7–9: "Therefore, so that I would not exalt myself, a thorn in the flesh was given to me, a messenger of Satan to torment me so that I would not exalt myself. Concerning this, I pleaded with the Lord three times that it would leave me. But he said to me, 'My grace is sufficient for you, for my power is perfected in weakness.'" Your thorn may be a physical ailment, constant financial pressure, or anxiety and depression. Whatever it is, God can use it to platform his power in the places where you just don't feel like you have what you need to perform, keep up, or survive.

Christians have for generations recognized the growth God brings from suffering in our lives. "How would the great work of sanctification go on in a man if he had no trial?" wrote the great J. C. Ryle in his book, *Holiness*. He goes on to write, "Trouble is often the only fire which will burn away the dross that clings to our hearts. Trouble is the pruning knife which the great Husbandman employs in order to make us fruitful in good works. The harvest of the Lord's field is seldom ripened by sunshine only."[3] Ryle's category of "trouble" includes our struggles with anxiety and depression. He goes on to write, "When days of darkness come upon us, let us not count it a strange thing. Rather let us remember that lessons are learned on such days, which would never have been learned in sunshine. Let us say to ourselves, 'This also is for my profit, that I may be a partaker of God's holiness. It is sent in love. I am in God's best school. Correction is instruction. This is meant to make me grow.'"[4]

Stewarding Your Pain

Most of us don't immediately think of our pain as something that can be stewarded. In our best-case scenarios, we may try to lament and grieve, find some healing, and hope to move on. But our pain as believers is valuable. At the least, it offers information and experience in living with hope through difficulty that can help us in future pain. But if stewarded well, our pain can be a huge resource for others as they walk through the many struggles of living in a fallen world.

Through our pain we learn of God's faithfulness, tenderness, and nearness. As Paul writes in 2 Corinthians 1:4, "He comforts us in all our affliction, so that we may be able to comfort those who are in any kind of affliction, through the comfort we ourselves receive from God." It's one thing to know God's kindness in the abstract and to remind others of it as they suffer. It's something entirely different to hear the voice of a person who has suffered the same kind of pain you are currently experiencing. Their encouragement and words of hope can bolster us like no one else's because they've come out the other side of the dark tunnel with God and his praise still on their lips. They know the deep fears and losses that come with our particular type of pain and can speak directly into them. I (Christine) have experienced this on both ends, as the one needing comfort and the one comforting. I have been amazed by God's use of my pain in multiple areas for the encouragement and consolation of others.

Stewarding Your Energy

When talking about limits, I often have my clients do a drawing activity to help them visualize their energy output. Before we begin, I explain that we all have energy coins that we get to spend in any given week. First, I have my client draw a square. In the middle of that square, they draw many small circles to represent the coins they have to spend on their God-given responsibilities. These are the essentials that cannot be compromised like kids, a spouse, or a chronic illness. These parts of their story aren't going anywhere and always need to be factored in. If they don't spend coins here, they'll cause all kinds of other issues.

Outside the box they draw small circles for all the responsibilities that come and go depending on the season they're in such as a job or a specific commitment. These circles may represent everything from membership in the PTA to tasks for a church committee or a home renovation or a bigger project at work or driving a child to a month full of more birthday parties than usual. Remember that these circles represent energy coins. We all have a limited number and must spend them wisely. And some of us might have more coins than others. In some seasons your health might need you to spend more coins on it than others, like during a difficult diagnosis. Some other responsibilities might demand more attention at times, like transitioning to a new role at work or addressing a specific marriage struggle. During those months or years, you'll need to draw a few more circles in your responsibility square, essentially transferring coins back from outside the square to the inside. This represents a redistribution of energy as the seasons and circumstances change.

This process provides a visual of the responsibilities in our lives. It helps my clients understand where they're spending their energy. This will ebb and flow. But the picture they draw helps people answer questions like: Am I spending fifteen coins in this area, or am I spending just one or two? Can I give more to the people outside the square? Or do my people inside the square need more from me right now? Using this exercise can help you remember and live more comfortably within your limits as you care for others.

Stewarding Wisdom

What is wisdom? And how is it involved with figuring out your anxiety and depression? Wisdom is a huge resource needed for any believer to help them learn how to manage their anxiety and depression. Wisdom is applying the Word of God to our lives in practical ways. He encourages us to ask him for this kind of wisdom in James when he says, "Now if any of you lacks wisdom, he should ask God—who gives to all generously and ungrudgingly—and it will be given to him" (James 1:5). We need God's insight in every area of life, even our mental health. Romans 11:33–34 reads, "Oh, the depth of the riches both of the wisdom and the knowledge of God! How unsearchable His judgments and untraceable *his ways! For who has known the mind of the Lord? Or who has been His counselor?*" (HCSB, emphasis added).

The Creator of all things knows all things about his creation. His wisdom and knowledge have a depth that far outreaches anything we will ever know or understand. So much so that we will never have to be his counselor, but he will always be ours. We must go to the Wisdom Giver and ask him how to spend our money, parent our children, move in and out of jobs, and treat our anxiety or depression.

But we also need to ask the Wisdom Giver how to steward our specific bodies. What does your body need to help you push back against the fall? What might trigger anxiety or depression in one person may not in another. We all have different stories, genetics, and heart idols that make each of us our own unique case. For instance, some people become sad when they're alone while others become sad when they don't have enough alone time. Some people feel anxious when they go to the grocery store while others are relaxed by it. We must go to God and ask him to give us wisdom about how to steward our bodies and their unique mix of characteristics. We ask for guidance about things like sleep patterns, medications, and what workload we can manage. If you're someone who struggles with seasonal affective disorder, wisdom might be saying no to living in a city with little opportunity for direct sunlight. Or, in another example, maybe you're trying to decide what day to have a root canal done. If you fight anxiety at the dentist, wisdom looks like making the appointment on a day when a friend can come with you or drive you.

Stewarding Your Life Rhythms and Anchors

Anxiety and depression can cause repeated patterns of behavior that disrupt our ability to live in healthy rhythms. Sometimes this can leave us feeling like anxiety or depression run the show, and we don't seem to have much control. We might feel as if we're always on the defense, responding to our mental health instead of being on offense and getting proactively ahead of it. When this happens, it feels like we're in a car with no brakes. Have you ever felt this way? We're going to introduce you to a concept that will help you make the shift to offense.

There are several life rhythms or "anchors" that can greatly change the way you deal with your anxiety or depression. These can also enable you to work within your "frame" as Psalm 139 calls it: the way you're put together and the fact that you're finite. When you think of an anchor, you imagine something that holds a ship in place no matter the water conditions around the boat. We are that boat, and God uses certain things to help hold us in place despite the conditions. Sleep, moving your body, fueling your body, and connecting with the Lord are key rhythms or anchors for mental health. When these four areas are moving in the right direction, they can be a huge stabilizer for us. Moving in the right direction doesn't mean that you need to be earning an A or a 100 percent on every anchor. Try shooting for a B or an 80 percent. Neglecting a certain anchor can cause a rise in depression or anxiety. This will differ from person to person. For example, some people might experience a spike in anxiety if they don't get the right amount of sleep. For others it might be movement. Take time to figure out which anchor is the one you need to watch the closest to stop your whole ship from floating out to sea.

Sleep is foundational for the body and something we often don't consider or talk about enough when it comes to mental health. Lack of sleep, interrupted sleep, and inconsistent sleep patterns can be like lighter fluid on an already burning fire.[5] The parts of your brain that help you be less anxious do not work as well when you lack sleep.[6] How many hours of sleep are you getting a night? What time do you go to bed? What time do you wake up? What do you do before you go to bed? These are just some helpful questions to ask to assess your sleep rhythms. Then you can change what's needed to anchor yourself down.

Moving your body is the second life rhythm or anchor. Our bodies are designed to move. Doing physical activity—whether walking, playing pickleball, lifting weights, gardening, or any other similar activity—helps produce endorphins in the brain, which increase feelings of happiness and reduce pain. While people disagree on what the most effective exercise is to make this happen, they all agree that moving your body makes it happen. If you're struggling with anxiety or depression, ask yourself questions about moving your body: How much activity am I getting each week? What types of exercise do I love? What types do I hate? What can I work into my weekly schedule and see if it impacts my mental health? You might be surprised by the help this life anchor brings.

Fueling your body is the third anchor for your mental health. This includes being watchful about what you eat, and we don't mean in a "diet, calorie-counting" kind of way. It means eating healthy foods—ones that make your body feel good (i.e., no stomachaches, reflux, or sluggishness after you eat them). They give you energy and make you feel filled up and ready to engage with what's next. Start to pay attention. What food makes you feel bad after you eat it? What food gives you a boost? Try to work those into your weekly meals and see how they affect your mood.

The final anchor for mental health is connection and time with the Lord. You might be thinking, *Isn't this the foundation of all mental health?* Yes, that's true. But these four areas must all be checked in their relationship to your anxiety and depression. When was the last time you spent time reading the Bible? How often are you praying and taking your fears and sadness to the Lord? Are you ever making the time to sit before him in silence? Survey this anchor and notice the impact your engagement with God or lack of it is having on your anxiety or depression.

Do Anxiety or Depression Disqualify Me?

If you've lived with clinical anxiety or depression, you know how difficult it can be not only for you but also for those who love you. Those close to you need to know how you struggle and how they can help you when needed. Sometimes you might wonder if it's overwhelming or unfair to ask someone to enter the immense struggle you have with one of these afflictions. Our closest relationships, specifically, can be impacted by mental health. For example, what impact could your anxiety or depression have on a marriage or children?

First, we must begin by saying none of these decisions are a hard and immediate yes or no. These are wisdom issues, just like figuring out how to steward our bodies or choose a career. Every person's situation is different and requires prayer and advice from multiple wise friends who love us. Second, honesty is the only path forward. Just as you would discuss your congenital heart disease or your childhood history with a potential spouse, so you need to talk practically about your anxiety or depression.

People often wonder about the impact of anxiety and depression on a marriage. How will chronic panic attacks look in my marriage?

How will having a hard time getting out of bed for weeks at a time impact my spouse or kids? Sometimes mental health issues are clear before you get married. Sometimes they're not. These are good things to talk through just as you would any other issues that limit your spouse's functioning and how they engage with the world around them. Pray and seek wisdom from the Lord and those who know and love you both. Explore what this could mean for your marriage and whether a long-term relationship would work.

Sometimes mental health issues, like so many other things, do not become apparent until after you're married. In these cases, you must approach the issue like you would any other suffering that impacts the relationship: with prayer, support, counseling, and wisdom from those who love you and love the Lord. You must recognize the real weight mental-health issues can place on your marriage dynamic. However, on the flip side these struggles can be the very things that God uses to sanctify you and your spouse. They can also grow you in connection to God and the body of Christ. Long-suffering with a spouse who struggles can teach you so much about your own weakness and need for the Lord. It can teach you how to pray. It can teach you how to allow other believers in your life to share the burden. It can teach you, ultimately, about all that Jesus, the Man of Sorrows, underwent when he "took up our infirmities and carried our sorrows" as God in the flesh (Isa. 53:4 BSB).

A client recently said to me (Hope), "What if I'm too anxious to have a baby?" This was a fair question from someone who is a lifelong struggler with anxiety. Just like the process you go through to discern the effect of mental health on a potential marriage, ask yourself similar questions before pursuing the growth of your family. There are no hard-and-fast rules here. The most important things in this process are: (1) Acknowledge that you have mental health issues. (2) Acknowledge that they impact all areas of life including this one. (3) Remember that God is always at work in our lives, even in places of struggle and suffering. Often in the combination of marriage, kids, and mental health, the outcome brings both good and bad. But if

God is calling you to either of these commitments, you can expect him to show up, equip, and sustain you.

What about ministry? Sometimes those who struggle with anxiety or depression question their fitness for vocational or even volunteer ministry. They may ask questions like, "How can I preach about the hope of the gospel if I struggle with hope myself?" Or, "How can I teach people about the peace a relationship with Jesus brings when I'm so often full of anxiety?" The answers to these questions depends on severity. But in general, the belief that any sort of weakness disqualifies us from ministry is based on a wrong view of the kingdom of God. God has worked through fragile, weak people throughout biblical history. Though he gives gifts by the Spirit and uses them for the building up of the church, he also shows his strength and the power of his gospel through our weakness.

Paul recorded God's answer to him when he asked that God might take away his "thorn," a place of weakness in his life: "But he said to me, "My grace is sufficient for you, for my power is perfected in weakness." Paul went on to categorize his weakness as a reason for boasting, that Christ's power might be platformed: "Therefore, I will most gladly boast all the more about my weaknesses, so that Christ's power may reside in me. So I take pleasure in weaknesses, insults, hardships, persecutions, and in difficulties, for the sake of Christ. For when I am weak, then I am strong" (2 Cor. 12:9–10). If a God-appointed apostle can boast about Jesus in the middle of severe weakness, we have hope to do the same.

Charles Spurgeon was known as the "Prince of Preachers" because of his incredibly powerful sermons. And Spurgeon struggled with debilitating depression most of his life. He owned many books on mental health and frequently wrote about it. He called himself a "prisoner" of depression. But Spurgeon's depression didn't hinder his ministry—in fact, it helped it. Spurgeon's pain gave him a great compassion for those he pastored.[7]

Consider William Cowper, Anglican hymn writer and poet. He wrote several powerful hymns including "There Is a Fountain Filled with Blood" and "God Moves in a Mysterious Way," which includes the following beloved verses:

> God moves in a mysterious way,
> His wonders to perform;
> He plants his footsteps in the sea,
> And rides upon the storm.
> Ye fearful saints fresh courage take,
> The clouds ye so much dread
> Are big with mercy, and shall break
> In blessings on your head.

This talented believer who gifted the church with well-crafted lines that encourage our faith struggled most of his life with depression. He attempted suicide multiple times and lived for a while in what was then termed an "insane asylum." While the severity of their affliction may alter how and when we minister—and at what pace—anxiety and depression do not disqualify us from ministry on a wholesale level. In fact, they are the very things God might use to give compassion for others and teach dependence on the One we serve.

Conclusion

Christians often talk about stewarding their money and even their time. But as believers, we steward *everything* God has given us. Joy and suffering, thorns and energy, limits and abilities, singleness and marriage. We seek God's wisdom in our stewardship and do our best to faithfully steward the bodies he has given us. We will never do these things perfectly. But whether we're stewarding our anxiety and depression, our free time, our possessions, or our student debt, we must remember who holds all things in his hands. The King of kings to whom we answer is not a cruel taskmaster or a harsh judge. Rather, he is a sympathetic and powerful priest. "For we do not have a high priest who is unable to sympathize with our weaknesses, but one who has been tempted in every way as we are, yet without sin.

Therefore, let us approach the throne of grace with boldness, so that we may receive mercy and find grace to help us in time of need" (Heb. 4:15–16). Approach Jesus's throne of grace often as you attempt to steward all He's given you. You'll find mercy and grace every time.

Questions for Reflection

1. How did this chapter introduce you to a new way of thinking regarding stewardship—whether that be God's or your own?

2. What areas of your life have you found difficult to steward regarding your mental health?

3. How are limitations a kindness from God? What limits do you need to accept?

4. What rhythm or anchor has the biggest impact on your mental health? What practical changes, if any, do you need to make in this area?

5. What decision are you trying to make about the impact of anxiety and depression on ministry, marriage, kids, or other categories? What new insight do you have from this chapter?

Chapter 9

Helping Those We Love

"Bear one another's burdens, and so fulfill the law of Christ."
Galatians 6:2 ESV

I (Hope) once read a story about a pastor from Nebraska who was sent to San Francisco with a job title of "the ministry of presence." His job was to walk the streets from 11:00 p.m. until 7:00 a.m. and care for the homeless, the prostitutes, and the destitute. He would often just be with them, even accompanying them to the hospital if they had a crisis or emergency. He was embodying the gospel. His ministry changed lives for Jesus. Never minimize what being present can do for someone who is struggling. Helping often starts with the simple, brave step of moving toward someone.

Over the years we have heard so many beautiful accounts of people loving depressed and anxious people well. Stories of friends cleaning people's houses, sitting with them in the dark for hours, praying over them in bed, going with them to the doctor, driving them to counseling, watching their kids, mowing their lawns, or dropping off flowers or coffee.

A few years ago, my (Hope's) aunt got into a terrible car accident. When I called my cousin, she was sitting at the ER waiting to find out if her mom would make it. She was later transferred to the ICU in St. Louis. I live all the way down in San Antonio and couldn't get to her. But Christine lives in St. Louis. She offered to be present with my family; she offered to go in my place. She brought my cousin food. She rubbed her shoulders, prayed with her, and even went into the room with my aunt. A few months ago, my aunt called me and said,

"Was your friend at the hospital after my accident? Because I'm just now remembering that she came by. And I can't tell you how loved I feel that she would do that." Christine didn't do much that day. But she moved toward the pain, and it mattered.

I (Christine) was attending a conference one summer where I was hosting a table for At His Feet Studies, the Bible study company Hope and I cofounded. It was mid-June, and I had just lived through a long cloudy May full of struggles with one difficult child and worries about another. I had zero energy and little motivation. And yet I was about to spend three days talking to hundreds of women about our books, attempting to convince them that what we had written would help them. Both Hope and my husband, Michael, were at the conference with me. Both had to help me get out of bed that week. Both reminded me at one point that my only job for the next few minutes was to put my shoes on because that's the only job I was capable of at that moment. They encouraged me, gave me long hugs, brought me food, and made me laugh. The only reason I talked to anyone that week was because of these two loving souls.

About four times over the last twenty-five years, my anxiety has gotten so bad that I (Hope) have had to be in bed for a day or two. When that happens, it's hard for me to eat, sleep, or work. Several times during these episodes, I have had friends come into my bedroom, sit on my bed, and pray for me. They often say, "We don't know what to say. You're usually the one who knows what to say. But we're here and we love you." I can still see their faces. I have felt so cared for; this was holy ground. I felt Jesus right there in my bedroom. Friends did countless other things: listened to all my irrational and rational fears, drove me to the store and the doctor, watched my kids, cooked me food. When I'm anxious, one of my fears is that I will almost "get lost" in my own mind. When people have helped me, I've felt less alone and less scared.

Jesus's Example

The pain of other humans is incredibly complex and storied. While we must always remember that no two people's experiences of anxiety or depression are alike, we can, with the help of the Holy Spirit, be a powerful help to those who struggle. Jesus's life is a template for an attitude that seeks to help those in pain: "Adopt the same attitude as that of Christ Jesus, who, existing in the form of God, did not consider equality with God as something to be exploited. Instead he emptied himself by assuming the form of a servant, taking on the likeness of humanity. And when he had come as a man, he humbled himself by becoming obedient to the point of death—even to death on a cross" (Phil. 2:5–8).

Jesus's response to our suffering was never to pull away or refuse to get his hands dirty. He put his rights and reputation aside. He left his place of comfort to enter into our dirty, broken, sad world. He got as close as he could to us and served.

Luke 7:11–17 tells the story of Jesus walking with his disciples and running into a funeral procession for the son of a widow. Instead of passing by this interruption, he saw and had compassion on the woman who had lost both her husband and her only son. He spoke to her, touched the coffin of the dead man, and healed him. "The dead man sat up and began to speak, and Jesus gave him to his mother" (v. 15). The result of this miracle? People glorified the Father and drew the right conclusion about Jesus's reason for being on this earth: "God has visited his people" (v. 16).

Just a chapter later in Luke 8:40–56, Jesus stopped amid a crowd when he felt power leave him. He made the woman who had been healed by the touch identify herself and then dignified her by calling her daughter and telling her she had been saved by her faith. He went from there to raise a young girl from the dead whose father had pleaded with him, falling at his feet earlier. When the little girl awoke from death, he commanded something—and it wasn't that she should immediately report to him all the evangelism strategies she would here forth employ or even that she rise and get to good kingdom work but "that she be given something to eat" (v. 55).

Jesus's response to our suffering is to enter into it. To come near it. To be the way God visits us in our woes and wailing, helping us along with a gentle touch or a warm meal. He did this in the lives of individuals he encountered while living here on earth. He did it for the world by dying on the cross as an innocent man. We attempt to enter into other people's suffering because Jesus first entered into ours. And when we do, God is not only glorified in a generic sense, but people are genuinely visited by him in their specific time of need.

How to Enter In

If you're reading this chapter, it's because you love people and you want to help them in their pain. Have you ever felt afraid or hesitant to get involved because you don't know how? Or maybe you're not sure what's helpful? Maybe you're not sure you have the skills or time to engage with the situation. It would be wonderful if there was a perfect way to help our suffering loved ones and boundless energy to do so. Neither of those things is reality. Remember how we talked about limits in chapter 8? Those things apply to you as a helper as well. You only have so many energy coins to spend. As you read about the forthcoming ways to help others, resist the urge to perform every single one of them simultaneously or to try to apply everything you learn at the same time. Pace yourself. Ask God for wisdom about where he wants you to spend the resources he's given you.

When people are suffering with anxiety and depression, it's helpful to think in two categories: spiritual encouragement and practical help.

Spiritual Encouragement

How can you help spiritually? First, there are words of hope given by God in Scripture that anxious and depressed hearts need to hear. A person amid a great struggle with anxiety or depression has often become unanchored from the truths that have tethered them to God in the past. Gently reminding them of a few basic truths can start to anchor them again spiritually. And I do mean gently. You might remind them that God is real and present with them. Perhaps you can share one of these: "And remember, I am with you always, to the end of the age" (Matt. 28:20). "When you pass through the waters, I will be with you" (Isa. 43:2).

They need to know he loves them: "No one has greater love than this: to lay down his life for his friends" (John 15:13). That he's not angry at them for feeling this way: "Therefore, since we have been justified by faith, we have peace with God through our Lord Jesus Christ" (Rom. 5:1). That he knows what suffering feels like: "He was despised and rejected by men, a man of suffering who knew what sickness was" (Isa. 53:3). That one day they will not feel like this: "He will wipe away every tear from their eyes. Death will be no more; grief, crying, and pain will be no more, because the previous things have passed away" (Rev. 21:4). And that their suffering is never wasted: "And not only that, but we also boast in our afflictions, because we know that affliction produces endurance, endurance produces proven character, and proven character produces hope" (Rom. 5:3–4).

Practical Help

Practical help will look different from spiritual encouragement, but it is just as important. These are the ways you get to enter into this person's situation and lighten their actual, tangible load. With both anxiety and depression, many daily tasks that make our lives run become difficult. Here are a few ideas to get your imagination going on how you might practically help:

- Do they need someone to cook them a meal?
- Do they need help mowing their yard or doing their laundry?
- Maybe they need regular childcare so they can go to counseling or doctors' appointments.
- They might need help paying for counseling.

- Maybe they need you to go for a walk with them or get them coffee and sit in silence.

When asking them what's helpful, get specific in what you can offer, giving them options to decide what is best. Asking them, "How can I help?" might be too broad or overwhelming for them to answer. Instead, give them specific options of help you can offer and let them choose what would feel most helpful to them with questions like, Can I do your dishes or take your kids to the park? This type of question also implies that you're in this with them and that you're committed to providing help. (And it also allows you to outline the kind of help you can genuinely offer in this season, given your own commitments and capacity.) By giving specific options, you can offer what you are able to while simultaneously hearing from them what the best help might be. Of course, if they really don't want any help, that's for them to decide as well.

Asking Questions: Speaking of questions, what a powerful tool for helping! Unfortunately, they're often underused. Using the tool of questions increases your ability to accurately, lovingly care for people in a way that is helpful for them. Sometimes we sit with people who are suffering and offer all kinds of statements or advice but hardly ask any questions. Sometimes people don't ask questions because they think, *If she wanted me to know how she is struggling, she would just tell me.* As a therapist (Hope), I'm here to tell you she most likely *won't.* Why? Because she feels shame, embarrassment, or like she's a burden in her current situation or struggle. People often keep their struggles with anxiety and depression to themselves and hesitate to share.

Using questions is a way for you to acknowledge that people are complex. Everyone has different life experiences, has lived in different parts of the world, and has come from a different type of family. Everyone has a different story. People are wired differently. Some are more feelers than thinkers. Some like to be vulnerable and some hate it. Some know what they're feeling when they're feeling it. Others have no clue. The differences are endless. While we have Christ in common, there are many layers in each of us. When we don't ask questions, it's usually because we assume we already know what a person is thinking and feeling. But do we really know? While we might be intuitive and wise, we might only be seeing part of the picture, not the whole picture. Before you spend time with someone you love who is struggling with anxiety or depression, think ahead about the questions you can ask. Of course, they always have the option not to answer. You can do that by saying something like, "It's totally fine if you don't feel comfortable answering this." If they don't answer, go back to just being present with them, spending time with them.

Here are a few helpful questions you can try: "What is on your mind today? What has been really weighing on you lately?"

When they start telling you about something hard, you can ask them: "How are you feeling about all of this?"

Or, "What thought keeps going through your mind when you think about this situation?"

Or, "What's your fear about this situation?" (This one always gets the most helpful answers. It's a great window into the heart, especially because we all fear different things.)

Or, "Where do you feel God is in all of this? What do you feel like he's up to?"

If you are someone who has struggled with anxiety or depression and you're going to care for someone who is struggling in a similar way, be careful. Just because you've been through something similar doesn't mean you know exactly how they feel. Instead of assuming, ask them how they feel. Be slow and prayerful about giving advice. Sometimes saying an unhelpful thing at the wrong time can feel more like adding a heavy burden to someone instead of lightening their load. Be prayerful about this. And apologize when you misstep.

Validation: Validation is another helpful tool for those who are struggling. This involves telling someone their opinions and feelings about a situation are *worthwhile* and *make sense*. Validation goes something like this: A woman at your church tells you she's been anxious and is having a hard time sitting all the way through a church service. Instead of trying to talk her out of how she's feeling or talk her into "looking on the bright side," start by validating her feelings.

Say something like this: "Thank you for sharing that with me. That sounds really hard! It makes sense that you feel that way." You will be amazed at how cared for and seen people will feel just by those small statements.

I know some of you are thinking, *Well, what if what they tell me doesn't sound hard? Or what if I think they're being ridiculous in getting worked up by that?* That's fair. It's true that when we hear people tell their stories, some seem harder than others. But the focus must be on how their circumstances feel to them. They are the ones currently living through this struggle. Your opinion about their situation is less important at that moment. Why? Because everyone feels difficulty in different ways and at different levels. What might feel hard for one person might not be a big deal for you. What might be a big deal for you might feel like a small problem to someone else. Regardless, a human is suffering on some level, and God cares about that. While we don't validate sin, we can always validate someone's struggle against sin or how difficult their suffering is. This is true whether they're suffering because of their own choices or the choices of others.

Back when I (Hope) was the women's director at church, I once was meeting with a woman who was feeling stuck and struggling with an issue. I noticed when she would bring it up to other women in Bible study and other settings they would usually start to give her lots of advice. They'd try to convince her that she should feel differently than she did. She would get more defensive or give a longer list of reasons she felt the way she did. One day as we were talking, I decided to take a different approach. When she brought up the subject, I listened and validated her feelings. I told her how hard her situation must be. When she expressed pain about it, I met her in it and agreed with her that it felt hard for her. She then started to acknowledge her role in the situation and talked about how she wanted to take responsibility for her part. I was shocked. I didn't have to get her to that conclusion. She got there on her own because I didn't try to fix her pain. I simply acknowledged how the situation was making her feel. I learned a lot that day. After that I used validation more often. I'm always surprised by the results.

Many times, people simply want to know you are *for* them before they admit the work they need to put in regarding a frustrating situation in their lives. Validating someone's feelings does not mean you let them stay in sin or condone wrongdoing. Validation is a meeting point on their side of the bridge so you might walk with them over it according to the pace of God's work in their heart.

Don't Leave Them Alone: Those who struggle with depression, especially, may push others away when they need their help. Being around others can feel like it takes more energy than a depressed person has. This can cause them to refuse help and even lead to a sort of reclusive existence. Don't let them fool you; this is not what they need. You may have to convince them to let you spend time with them. Once you do, don't require conversation or much activity. Your presence tells them they matter, and their depression is not too much for others. You might offer things you know they enjoy—a good meal, a walk, time with an animal, or time in a favorite place. Even if they refuse all things, make clear to them that they're important to you and that they don't need to do anything for you. Your presence matters. Richard Baxter, puritan pastor who spent many hours and days with depressed people, gave the following instructions for those caring for people struggling with depression: "Intrude into their space. . . . Don't allow them to spend too much time alone, but arrange for suitable companions to be with them, or take them to visit friends."[1]

What's Not Helpful

Many who struggle with anxiety and depression have had well-meaning friends or family try to help only to make things harder. Anxious or depressed people are not helped by quick advice or suggestions. "You know, my aunt started taking a thirty-minute walk every day, and it really helped her mood. You should try that." Or, "Ooh, you need that new breathing technique they're teaching the kids at school!" These suggestions might eventually be things your friend needs. But jumping in with advice without listening first or validating their feelings can actually make someone feel even more lonely than they already are in their suffering.

Your friend also will not be helped by "one up" stories. "You think that's bad? One time my friend at work was so depressed she didn't get out of bed or eat for three days." Or, "You know, I'm probably worse. I can't even ride in an elevator because I get so anxious." Your desire in sharing these things is likely because you're making a warm-hearted attempt to relate to them or help them feel understood. But most times, this approach ends up minimizing their pain and leaves them to again feel more alone in it.

One last thing that's not helpful? Attempting to diagnose the root cause of their struggle. As someone close to them, you may be able to say some discerning things about what you've seen in their life that they haven't. You might remind them of something they've been through before or a season of life they've forgotten. But definitive statements about simplistic causes won't help them. "You know, you're anxious because your sister is coming. You really shouldn't let her stay with you." Or, "Those murder stories you read are making you depressed." As mentioned before, asking questions will help your friend slowly discover the root of what's happening more than an enlightened pronouncement.

Caring as a Limited Human

You've probably heard of support groups for caregivers of the chronically ill, the dying, and the addicted. Helping takes time, energy, and emotional bandwidth. If you happen to be made by God with a big, empathetic heart, you might find yourself caring for more and more people or spending more and more hours with one or two friends who are really struggling. Remember that you, too, have limits and struggles and that it's not your job to take on the entirety of your friend or family member's struggle. Your loved one needs various kinds of helpers in their journey, not just you. Making sure you get the sleep, fuel, community, and connection to God that you need every day is not selfish. It's part of maintaining your ability to care for the person in front of you.

While we're made in God's image, we're different from him. We're limited. We can't help everyone with everything. We don't know all things, see all things, or have unlimited time, energy, or resources. You need to assess yourself as you attempt and plan to help women around you. Ask yourself these questions:

> "What types of situations overwhelm me?"
>
> "What number of interactions in a day make me feel anxious?"
>
> "When do I need to refer someone I'm caring for to a professional counselor because the things they want to talk about feel beyond my scope?"
>
> "When do I need to get others involved at my church so I don't get swallowed up into a situation that has more need than I can handle?"

Pray about this. Talk to those in your community. Ask the Holy Spirit to guide you as you minister to others. Remind yourself that you're just one of God's many tools to help others; you aren't the only one. Identify your limits and boundaries when helping, and stick to them as best you can.

When to Get More Help

Sometimes when we're helping others, we can be unsure of when to get more people involved. If you're helping someone who goes to your church, it would be wise to see what resources your church has to offer them. Is there a pastor they could meet with who can encourage them in the Lord while they struggle? Does your church offer financial help for counseling or have a suggested list of counselors? Is there someone in the church who has walked through anxiety and depression and would be willing to meet and offer care and prayer? Is there someone in the body who loves making meals and stopping in for regular visits? Getting that extra support from the church for the person struggling can be a huge gift to them and relief to you.

Sadly, sometimes someone you love or are caring for, whether that's a family member or a friend, might struggle with suicidal ideation. This can feel overwhelming and scary as you try to figure out how to care for them. Since you're not a mental health professional, it's not your job to screen them and assess what level of a threat they are to themselves. Your job is to get them to someone who can. You can do this by taking them to the local emergency room. If they have a therapist, you can reach out and ask them for instructions on what is best. It's important that while you're doing this you don't leave your friend or loved one alone. Also, if they've informed you of specific plans, you should remove any of these objects: a gun, medications, knives, ropes, and so on. You can call or text the Suicide and Crisis Lifeline (currently 988) for help at any time.

We want to leave you with one final thought. Often people try to figure out what makes a great counselor. Is it the most cutting-edge techniques? Is it that they know all the latest methods or research? While all these things are important, what those who study these things have found over and over is that it's the relationship between the client and counselor that makes the difference. The client needs to know that their counselor is a safe person to talk to who cares for them. This sounds a lot like discipleship and mentorship, doesn't it? If you don't remember anything else, remember that simply having a genuine, connected relationship with someone offers a huge amount of care. It's good soil for the Holy Spirit to grow something in. Ask him to guide you in this journey and remind you often that you're probably doing much more for your friend than you think!

Questions for Reflection

1. How does Jesus enter the lives of suffering people? What does being present with them look like?

2. What did you learn from this chapter about asking questions? What is a specific question you want to start using when caring for others?

3. What did you learn about validation from this chapter? In what specific relationships do you want to try and practice this skill?

4. What boundaries or limitations do you have in your helping? If you don't have any currently, make some time this week to create a list. Doing this will help you last longer in your friendships instead of burning out.

5. In what type of situations do you need to get more help? Where do you currently need to consider doing this?

Chapter 10

The Glory That Is Coming

"Then I heard a loud voice from the throne: Look, God's dwelling is with humanity, and he will live with them. They will be his peoples, and God himself will be with them and will be their God. He will wipe away every tear from their eyes. Death will be no more; grief, crying, and pain will be no more, because the previous things have passed away. Then the one seated on the throne said, 'Look, I am making everything new.'"

Revelation 21:3–5

When was the first time you were taught about heaven? What did you visualize it looking like, or what did others tell you would be there? Heaven. It's a word often mentioned but not always understood. Many believers have tried to shape a picture in their minds of what our future reality will be. This is also true for anxious and depressed saints as they walk out life here, trying to draw on this future reality.

Do Anxious and Depressed People Feel the Same Way About Heaven?

Often, they don't. When anxious people think of life after death, they can be filled with a rush of feelings and racing thoughts: *What will it feel like? Will it hurt? Will I have a panic attack along the way?* New situations tend to unlock new potential fears for people who are anxious. The idea of heaven is no different. Sometimes when I (Hope) talk in my office about the hope of heaven, my anxious clients feel tense, hesitant to imagine it, and usually ask, "How does that help me now?"

On the other hand, depressed people tend to engage with the idea of heaven in a practical, helpful way as few people can. A place to rest and experience joy forever is exactly what a depressed person is looking for. For some it can even increase their suicidal ideation because they'd love to arrive in heaven sooner and escape their current pain.

Both depressed and anxious believers have gotten many things right and lots of things wrong about heaven. Many of us don't have a biblically informed imagination of heaven. Why does that even matter? Because we might be neglecting a tool that God has fashioned to help keep us afloat, comforted, and energized for living here in the time between right now and when we get to glory (also called the "already-not-yet" by many Christian thinkers). A full and correct vision of heaven can be an amazing motivator or calming influence for those who most need it. But how do we begin to inform such a vision? Not with strange ideas of otherworldly creatures and landscapes but by hoping for even more of the goodness we know here on earth.

Setting My Mind on Things Above with Things Below

When I (Christine) think of earthly things that make me happy beyond belief, Bach's *Mass in B Minor* immediately comes to mind. But there are so many others: the house finches feeding outside my window; the lush green that's beginning to fill my yard again; Satchmo, the large and beautiful white dog I've watched grow from puppyhood across the street; and his kind and funny owner, Janice. Add to the list Mexican street tacos; hikes with a view; and fresh-smelling, warm towels out of the dryer. Not to mention Steinbeck novels, simple crochet patterns, and raised-bed gardens. And of course, long walks with friends, thoughtful discussions with colleagues, laughs with sisters, and hugs with a six-foot-three-inch son who holds on as long as I ask.

You, reader, could make your own list. It would be different from mine but just as lovely and full of goodness. And so a disconnect often comes for us when we begin to talk about life after death as some disembodied, cloudlike, ethereal place where we spend our entire day floating around like translucent cherubs with harps. Through sermons, music, and art, some of us have been taught that the next life is one devoid of sensory experience, except for the sound of praise music and maybe the wind on our faces from the occasional rustle of an angel's wings. No wonder we're not excited about where we're going: It doesn't sound very human.

Good News: You're Not Going to (Only) Heaven

If we spend some time investigating a biblical view of our eventual home, we'll find encouraging news. The truth about our final destination and final form as believers is such good news, in fact, that it can begin to transform our present lives. Instead of housing our future hope in "heaven," the Bible repeatedly tells us our final home is actually earth—but not the current version of it. It will be a new earth. Heaven will come down and meet earth, and our eternities will be spent on a remade, redeemed earth that has some continuity with the one we live on now.

One way to say it is that you're not going to heaven forever. Your soul will go to heaven when you die, yes, but once your soul reunites with your body in the coming resurrection, you will rise from the grave as a physical being and inhabit a renewed, physical world. Just as bodies undergo resurrection, so will this earth! So you're not staying in a spirit-only world, or heaven-only world, for the rest of eternity. You're eventually going to dwell within *heaven on earth*—both made new, both joined together, both in each other's space forever and ever amen.

Volumes have been written about what happens at the moment of death for a believer. More volumes have been written about how history will progress during the time between Jesus's resurrection and the final home for his people. While a deep dive into those might be interesting and encouraging, we want to equip you with things that spur you on. Our purpose here is not to discuss the details of the end time but to give hope and provision for the holy imagination of those currently suffering from anxiety and depression. Therefore, we'll leave topics like paradise, the intermediate state, and Gehenna for other books, and move toward life in the new earth.

If you're a Christian, your future reward is not some ghostly cloud-sitting and an endless choir practice. It's a full-bodied immersive experience including all the things you love about the earth now, only better. It's long, green hikes with forest views on national park trails but without the mosquito bites and muscle aches. It's seven-course meals with perfectly cooked risotto and delicately prepared lady fingers but without the high blood pressure or relational tension around the table. It's all the good of the earth magnified without the effects of the fall.

What can we know for sure about the future for those who belong to Jesus? A few things:

- We will live forever on a redeemed, restored earth (Isa. 26:19; 65:17, 21–23; Matt. 19:28; John 11:25; 2 Pet. 3:13; Rev. 21:1–4).
- We will inhabit resurrected, glorious bodies free of physical and emotional pain, distortion, and decay (Isa. 25:8; 65:19–20; Rom. 8:1–11; 1 Cor. 15:20, 42–54).
- We will be with Jesus and know him in his fullness (Luke 23:43, 1 Thess. 4:14; 2 Tim. 2:11–13; Rev. 21:7).
- We will be like Jesus, fully mature in our love for him and others (Rom. 8:29; 1 Cor. 3:18; Eph. 1:3–14; Phil. 1:6; 3:21; 1 John 3:2–3).
- We will celebrate, feast, and delight to work for him (Isa. 25:6–9; 65:21; Luke 19:11–27; Rev. 19:1–8; 22:3).

The promise of a new city that dwells on a renewed earth is throughout the Scriptures. John records his vision of this future in Revelation 21:1–2: "Then I saw a new heaven and a new earth; for the first heaven and the first earth had passed away, and the sea was no more. I also saw the holy city, the new Jerusalem, coming down out of heaven from God, prepared like a bride adorned for her husband." From heaven comes a city, a picture repeated in other passages. Revelation 21:10–12 reads, "He then carried me away in the Spirit to a great, high mountain and showed me the holy city, Jerusalem, coming down out of heaven from God, arrayed with God's glory. Her radiance was like a precious jewel, like a jasper stone, clear as crystal. The city had a massive high wall, with twelve gates. Twelve angels were at the gates; the names of the twelve tribes of Israel's sons were inscribed on the gates." Here we get more detail about the city, including a description of its wall and gates.

This is the city the faithful expect to find at the end of time perched within "a new earth, where righteousness dwells" (2 Pet. 3:13). Even Abraham was moving toward this city. Hebrews 11:10 reads, "For he was looking forward to the city that has foundations, whose architect and builder is God." And Abraham wasn't alone in this. Able, Enoch, Noah, Sarah—all of them "confessed that they were strangers and exiles on the earth. For those who say such things make it clear that they are seeking a country of their own. And indeed if they had been thinking of that country which they left, they would have had opportunity to return. But as it is, they desire a better country, that is, a heavenly one. Therefore God is not ashamed to be called their God; for He has prepared a city for them" (Heb. 11:13–16 NASB). Revelation 21:23–26 tells us this city doesn't need the sun because of the light of God's glory, its gates never shut, and all nations bring their "glory" into it.

Why does any of this matter now for the anxious or depressed person? Because your final destination has a huge impact on your present day. If weekends were a miserable, boring affair, no one would look forward to them. But Tuesday morning workloads are tackled partly with the hope of a Friday night meal with friends or a Saturday afternoon thrifting trip. How you view your life in eternity can offer great hope and comfort during the years you suffer on this earth, but only if you know what's coming.

So, what's so great about your living arrangements in eternity? And how does it move the needle for a depressed or anxious person? The new earth will feature everything that's great about earth now, only multiplied. The terrible effects of the fall that have touched every nook and cranny of the creation, including us, will be gone. Gone. There will be no death, stink, or blight. The anxiousness that plagued your brain with a heightened sense of alert—gone. The depression that dragged your head and heart into despair—finished. What you have lived in and under in regard to your mental health will no longer rule or reign. Redemption will.

The Bible tells the story not of annihilation but of redemption, not of destroying the earth altogether but of totally remaking the one that already exists. Think of a caterpillar becoming a butterfly. The caterpillar isn't destroyed but is transformed into something that seemed unimaginable in the worm stage. As one Christian thinker says, "Redemption doesn't mean scrapping what's there and starting again from a clean slate but rather liberating what has come to be enslaved."[1] All of the calming influence of a walk by a quiet brook or an hour in a park watching the birds will not only still be available but will be multiplied by glory. The encouragement and excitement of the crowd at a concert will be just as exhilarating but enhanced by total redemption. We can use our holy imaginations to begin to grow our anticipation of such pleasures, reminding ourselves that the current struggles we live in are not our forever home.

Our Resurrection Bodies

If you look up "resurrection body" online these days, the search will yield everything from an image of a glowing Jesus to a limp woman being sucked into a hole in the sky. Is there a way to narrow down the possibilities for our future? Thankfully, yes. Just as the Bible speaks in multiple places about the particulars of the new earth, so it records descriptions of our new bodies. First Corinthians 15:52–53 tells us, "For the trumpet will sound, and the dead will be raised incorruptible, and we will be changed. For this corruptible body must be clothed with incorruptibility, and this mortal body must be clothed with immortality." God is going to change our bodies that are capable of death into bodies that can never die. Just as the earth will be transformed and made new, so will our bodies. Just as the new earth will have continuity with the old, so will our bodies.

Chapter 32 of the Westminster Confession helps us here as it states, "At the last day, such as are found alive shall not die, but be changed; and all the dead shall be raised up with the self-same bodies, and none other, although with different qualities, which shall be united again to their souls forever."[2] While we don't know exactly what this means for our inseam (I hope for two more inches) or our singing voice (I hope to sound Grammy worthy), we do know these will be immortal. No decay or death will be able to touch them. No disease, deformation, or anything that is the result of the fall will mark these glorious bodies. This means no panic attacks, no tightening of the chest from sudden anxiety, no lack of energy or motivation caused by depression, and no wondering all day, *When can I just get back in bed?*

Think back to chapter 3 and our discussion of the extensive effects of the fall. Recall the scores of bodily systems that no longer work the way they were created to work. Neurotransmitters that our brains need to feel good fail to be produced. Our parasympathetic nervous system doesn't calm us down like it should. Our limbic system doesn't regulate our emotions. And on and on and on. These distorted and decaying bodies are all we've ever known. But our bodily resurrection will come with the ability to produce all the neurotransmitters we need to make us feel fantastic. Our parasympathetic nervous system will do its job lickety-split! Our limbic system will process our emotions just as it was intended to.

But also consider something more: The threats we encounter every day that cause our fight, flight, freeze, or fawn reactions will no longer exist. No danger will send our nervous system into a cascade of protective measures because no danger will exist. The whole "gates will never shut" thing in God's new city? Think about it: City gates have no need of shutting when there are no night shadows to fear—nor any hostile invaders creeping in with harmful motives. All that will be gone. We will live each moment in absolute safety, with all the opportunity and possibility of a whole, healed human. Every single system, organ, and cell that was affected by the fall will be renewed by the resurrection. Everything that went wrong with our bodies will be made right.

The continuity between our bodies on earth now and our resurrected bodies also means more good news: We'll recognize one another. Consider Jesus's appearance to the disciples in John 21. Peter and a few disciples were unsuccessfully fishing when a man on the shore told them to cast their net on the right side of the boat. When their nets were overwhelmed with fish, John recognized him. Jesus used his resurrected body to cook them a meal. "When they got out on land, they saw a charcoal fire there, with fish lying on it, and bread" (John 21:9). Jesus then ate some bread and shared it with them. Jesus didn't magically make a meal appear, nor did he feed them and skip breakfast. He used his physical body to cook and then ate a meal himself.

Thomas's doubts about Jesus's resurrection were not quieted until he was able to put his hand in his Savior's side. John 20:27 reads, "Then he said to Thomas, 'Put your finger here and look at my hands. Reach out your hand and put it into my side. Don't be faithless, but believe.'" Jesus's same hands, which were pierced with nails on the cross, served fish to the disciples on the beach. We can assume his resurrected body had the same face, voice, and shape as his predeath body. Since Jesus is the firstfruits of a new race (1 Cor. 15:20), what happens to him happens to us. As he goes, so we go. Therefore, we can expect continuity in our resurrected bodies. We should expect to recognize one another and to pick back up relationally with others the way he did with his disciples.

Why does this matter for those battling anxiety and depression now? The effort you make to invest in relationships now, even as you push back against your anxiety and depression, will pay glorious dividends in the future. It means the people we know, love, and enjoy who are saved on this fallen earth will be the people we know, love, and enjoy on the renewed earth. It means the shared stories, connection, and familiarity we treasure with friends and family will be present in our next life. Though marriage will not be a part of the new earth (Mark 12:25), rich relationships and memories will. Your "people"—the ones who make you laugh, the ones you hold dear—will still be your people in the new earth, along with plenty of other new friends you'll likely meet and enjoy. The point is this: You won't be starting over, lonely and struggling to make friends. Christ, your truest friend, will be a companion for the ages, along with all those in him—including the dearly loved ones you knew before.

Will Our Resurrection Bodies Remember Past Pain, Anxiety, or Depression?

This also means that some memory of past pain might exist but only as stories of victory. Paul forecasts some of this in 2 Corinthians 4:17–18: "For our momentary light affliction is producing for us an absolutely incomparable eternal weight of glory. So we do not focus on what is seen, but on what is unseen. For what is seen is temporary, but what is unseen is eternal." The scars visible to others will lead to the telling of battle stories that have been won by Christ in us, and pain that has been healed by him, too. We see this happening in Revelation 15:3, when all those gathered around God's heavenly throne sing the song of Moses and the song of the Lamb, remembering God's great deeds of deliverance from hardship into glory and from crucifixion to celebration. In another Revelation scene, the memory of Jesus being slain is remembered in heaven but only to celebrate God's incredible power not only to ransom his people but to invite them to reign with him (Rev. 5:8–14).

This means that we will likely retain our memories of transformation, of the way we were and of what we have become by the grace of God. Paul tells the Ephesians to remember who they were in Ephesians 2:11–12: "So, then, remember that at one time you were Gentiles in the flesh—called 'the uncircumcised' by those called 'the circumcised,' which is done in the flesh by human hands. At that time you were without Christ, excluded from the citizenship of Israel, and foreigners to the covenants of promise, without hope and without God in the world."

But the remembering is only for the purpose of thanking and worshipping God for what he has done. Paul goes on in Ephesians 2:13–14, "But now in Christ Jesus, you who were far away have been brought near by the blood of Christ. For he is our peace, who made both groups one and tore down the dividing wall of hostility."

Paul reminds the Corinthians of their past in 1 Corinthians 6:9–11: "Don't you know that the unrighteous will not inherit God's kingdom? Do not be deceived: No sexually immoral people, idolaters, adulterers, or males who have sex with males, no thieves, greedy people, drunkards, verbally abusive people, or swindlers will inherit God's kingdom. And some of you used to be like this," only to juxtapose these things with Christ's work: "But you were washed, you were sanctified, you were justified in the name of the Lord Jesus Christ and by the Spirit of our God." In other words, Paul is saying: "Remember your story of salvation, my friends. But not in a way that stagnates in sorrow and regret; rather in a way that celebrates the transformation you went through by the power of God and the sacrifice of Christ."

Do you see what Paul is doing? He is basically telling us to do now on earth what is already being done in heaven by those already present there (and will one day be done by *you* when you get there). Remember how the slain Lamb became the risen Lord. Remember how you, too, go through the pangs of weakness here and now but will be raised to glory just as Christ was. Look back, yes, but only to glory in how far God's brought you up to this point and where he's taking you next. Scars may be present in heaven but not to invite us into sorrow—rather, to compel us to sing.

This means that on the new earth, tales of past anxieties and sins—framed around Jesus's victory over them—might be told around campfires with exquisite s'mores and perfect fellowship. Hearts free of the weight of depression may celebrate God's complete joy and healing by recounting stories of God's faithfulness with an excellent meal at a table full of old friends. The people of God will have stories to tell, and each one will make us glory in God's victory over past struggles even more than the last.

Our Lives in Eternity

So, apart from the possibility of telling our victory stories around campfires, what will we be doing in this new earth with all our hours and days? How will we be using our resurrection bodies? We've talked some about the redeemed earth we'll enjoy. We should expect to do all the things we enjoy now: hike trails, fly fish, crochet soft blankets, shop for antique furniture, cook comfort food, and read incredible novels. We should also expect to work. Now, before your heart drops with disappointment, slow down for a minute and think about the things you dislike about your work on this earth. Whatever you spend your hours doing, it's fraught with problems, frustrations, and inefficiencies brought about by the fall. Copy machines break, software fails, and team members don't see eye to eye. Projects don't turn out the way we'd hoped. Grant money runs out. Not to mention all the ways your mental health has affected your view on work and you as a worker.

But here's the thing: Work was actually one of the things instituted by God *before* the fall. Work is not a result of the fall but was terribly tarnished by the fall. The curse did not create the category of work; fun, enlivening, meaningful, fulfilling work was already there. The curse introduced *painful toil* in our work (Gen. 3:17). All our good labor would find things choking back its productiveness and fruitfulness. Meaning, the only work we've ever known has been hindered by broken parts, damaged relationships, and distracted brains.

Imagine what would be possible for humans to build or create without the frustrations brought by the results of sin. Think about the work of a farmer. Before even planting, he has to make corrections in the soil so the pH level is correct as well as the composition. He has to remove rocks and weeds, till the soil, and amend the land to protect the soil from erosion. After all that work, his plants could still be damaged by hail, eaten by bugs, or ruined by drought. He has to factor in so much toil, and so many threats around the work of farming, to simply get things to grow.

Randy Alcorn writes, "Since the Fall, generations have lived and died after spending most of their productive years eking out an existence in the pursuit of food, shelter, and protection against theft and war. Mankind has been distracted and debilitated by sickness and sin."[3] There is no work that has not been adversely affected by sin's destruction.

Now imagine the farmer on the new earth where the crop yields won't be hindered by death or disease. His output and satisfaction in his work will be 100 percent at all times. He will use his imagination and learning to engineer new farming methods and new varieties of crops. But he won't fear failure or pressure from the bank. Think about what that could mean for other kinds of work. Teachers, artists, chefs, and architects, scientists, engineers, interior decorators, and orchardists will all be able to build and create, grow and tend without hindrance. Occupations like nursing, physical therapy, counseling, and dentistry will be completely obsolete, as the effects of the fall they work to push back on will no longer exist.

This future work has implications for what you do with your body today. Your work now will last into the future and be built on there. Revelation 14:13 says of Christians that, on their death and then entry into the next life, "their works follow them." Or, as Randy Alcorn puts it, "Just as we will be carried over from the old world to the new, so will our labor. In a sense, not only our bodies but our service for Christ will be resurrected."[4] Why does this change things for the depressed person? Because your work here, which can feel so meaningless and unmotivating, matters. All the anxiety you had to push through to get the job done was worth it in the end as the work was work that lasts! The skills and abilities you're building on now will be carried into the new earth for God-glorifying, joyful, fulfilling work.

The good work we do here may even be rewarded with more responsibility, again with constant satisfaction. In Matthew 25:14–30 Jesus tells the parable of the talents where the faithful work and management of certain people is rewarded with even larger amounts of responsibility. Some would interpret this parable to tell us that faithful management and work here on the fallen and decaying earth will be rewarded with more projects and responsibility in the new earth. Scripture gives us hints about a few other things we'll be doing: judging angels (1 Cor. 6:2–3), worshipping (Rev. 5:13), serving God (Rev. 22:3), receiving rewards (2 Cor. 5:10), and enjoying "a feast of rich food for all peoples, a banquet of aged wine—the best of meats and the finest of wines" (Isa. 25:6 NIV). None of these activities will include a single moment of anxiety or sadness. Revelation 21:4 reads, "He will wipe away every tear from their eyes. Death will be no more; grief, crying, and pain will be no more, because the previous things have passed away." This is made possible because, as John tells us in Revelation 22:3, "There will no longer be any curse."

The Best Part

You might think after all we've discussed that you've heard the best news about your future—not even close. Stunning art, scrumptious food, and amazing architecture—even in their perfection—still pale in their beauty compared to the astonishing splendor and ever-renewing thrill of being near Jesus. Have you ever felt the presence of Jesus? Maybe in a worship service or when being loved well by a friend? Whatever you've felt or seen, heard or experienced, it's only been a foretaste of the feast that's coming, a small window into the full panorama of Christ's overwhelming love for you. There will be no doubts as to whether he loves you or even if he likes you. You'll never wonder if he's mad or why he's allowing the pain that's come into your life. But beyond that, you'll never reach the end of his beauty or become bored with his character or personality. As J. C. Ryle wrote, "There are unsearchable riches in Christ's person."[5] The biggest joy of the new earth will be discovering those riches little by little, year after year.

Jonathan Edwards spoke of the future experience of enjoying God in a sermon delivered in 1733. He declared, "Better than fathers and mothers, husbands, wives or children, or the company of any, or all earthly friends. These are but shadows; but the enjoyment of God is the substance. These are but scattered beams; but God is the sun. These are but streams; but God is the fountain. These are but drops; but God is the ocean."[6] We will never grow tired of God, never be bored with who he is. As the psalmist wrote, "In your presence is abundant joy; at your right hand are eternal pleasures" (Ps. 16:11). If you thought Simone Biles's comeback in the 2024 Olympics to win all-around gold in gymnastics was amazing, or if you were wowed the first time your heard your favorite musician sing, wait until you experience a Tuesday afternoon with Jesus and the saints on a redeemed earth.

And what about relationships among one another? What will relating to other redeemed people be like in this new world? First, let's talk about what they won't be. You know that feeling you get around a good friend when you've been enjoying his company but suddenly notice a slightly uncomfortable look on his face after something you said? And now you're gripped with fear that he might reject you? Or that terrible weight on your chest that comes when your coworker says something that hurts you and makes you feel like a failure? Or that disorienting feeling that comes when you realize someone has lied to you? None of those scenarios will have a place in heaven. Instead, all relationships will be satisfying and good. Jealousy, envy, and fear won't exist. You'll never worry about what someone thinks about you, your family, or your work.

Just as the delight you find in Jesus will never end in the new earth, the same is true about the joy you'll find in your relationships with others. Again, Edwards is helpful: "Love in heaven is always mutual. It is always met with answerable returns of love with returns that are proportioned to its exercise . . . and in heaven this desire of love, or this fondness for being loved, will never fail of being satisfied."[7]

Holy Imagination

So, what might a Thursday afternoon look like on the new earth? Of course we can't know for sure, but we can, with our biblically informed imagination like we discussed in chapter 6, grow our anticipation of and lessen our anxiety about our lives in eternity. Maybe you meet an old friend for coffee at your favorite new cafe in Paris and listen to some of their stories about how Jesus gave them strength to care for their earthly husband as he died of cancer. But during your conversation, instead of worrying about whether your last question made her uncomfortable, you'll feel a connection to her that is stronger than any you felt while living on earth. You'll fully hear her story and be once again moved to tears by the goodness of God and the profound peace you feel in sitting with her.

Maybe you'll then stroll through Paris and stop into a patisserie to try some fresh bread. But while biting into your baguette, the flavors will be stronger and more lovely than any loaf you ever knew in the past, and you won't have a single thought of the calories you're consuming. Perhaps you'll order in French to practice the new language you're learning and think about where you might like to spend the next one hundred years, without a single fear of loneliness or danger. You might check in with your new group of good friends whom you've met while living in France and enjoy the energy and contentment you feel while walking through the clean streets of Paris.

From Pain to Glory

We began this book with misunderstanding, confusion, and pain. So many of us have misunderstood the nature of anxiety and depression and how God might have us fight back against them. We've also *been* misunderstood as we've tried to do so. We've known the confusion of living with real faith in Jesus but still struggling with anxiety and/or depression. All the pain brought about by the fall in the form of mental illness is real, tragic, and difficult. It must be acknowledged, lamented, and talked about with those we love and trust. Help is available, and Jesus is near those who suffer.

But your anxiety and depression are not the final word. They don't define who you are or who you will be. The God who knit you together and stays near to you all your life has given you ways to push back against the effects of the fall, to fight the darkness, to find healing and wholeness. And every step toward healing, every therapy session that brings clarity and shift, every medication that enables your brain to work a little more like it was meant to is a foretaste of heaven. Because heaven will bring endless days of healing, wholeness, and joy. On the new earth, your body will function just the way it was meant to function. Look to Jesus, dear one, and his resurrected body. He is your older brother, the firstborn of an entirely new kind of person. Your future is bound up in him, and your future is glorious.

Questions for Reflection

1. What ideas did you have about heaven before reading this chapter? Where did those ideas come from?

2. What was the biggest surprise to you about our lives in eternity? Why?

3. How does deepening your view on the new heavens and the new earth change how you engage with your anxiety and depression in this life?

4. How has your view on anxiety and depression been changed by reading this book? What are a few of your main takeaways?

Notes

Chapter 1

1. American Psychiatric Association, "American Adults Express Increasing Anxiousness in an Annual Poll; Stress and Sleep Are Key Factors Impacting Mental Health," May 1, 2024, https://www.psychiatry.org/News-room/News-Releases/Annual-Poll-Adults-Express-Increasing-Anxiousness.

2. "Prevalence of Major Depressive Episode Among Adolescents," National Institute of Mental Health, accessed August 21, 2025, https://www.nimh.nih.gov/health/statistics/major-depression.

3. "Prevalence of Major Depressive Episode Among Adolescents."

4. "Mental Health," World Health Organization, accessed August 21, 2025, https://www.who.int/news-room/fact-sheets/detail/mental-health-strengthening-our-response.

5. "Anxiety Disorders," National Institute of Mental Health, accessed August 21, 2025, https://www.nimh.nih.gov/health/topics/anxiety-disorders.

6. Mayo Clinic, "Depression," accessed December 9, 2024, https://www.mayoclinic.org/diseases-conditions/depression/symptoms-causes/syc-20356007.

Chapter 2

1. Derek Kidner, *Genesis* (InterVarsity Press, 1967), 50.

2. Anthony Hoekema, *Created in God's Image* (Eerdmans, 1994), 79.

3. Hoekema, *Created in God's Image*, 14.

4. Diana Wells, "21 Fun Facts About the Brain," Healthline, July 6, 2017, https://www.healthline.com/health/fun-facts-about-the-brain#21-fun-facts-about-the-brain.

5. Cleveland Clinic, "Oxytocin," accessed October 29, 2025, https://my.clevelandclinic.org/health/articles/22618-oxytocin.

6. Hoekema, *Created in God's Image*, 77.

Chapter 3

1. O. Köhler, J. Krogh, O. Mors, M. E. Benrosc, "Inflammation in Depression and the Potential for Anti-inflammatory Treatment," *Curr Neuropharmacol* 14, no. 7 (2016): 732–42.

2. G. J. Diefenbach, J. W. Goethe, "Does TMS Hold Promise for Generalized Anxiety Disorder?," accessed August 23, 2025, https://www.psychiatrictimes.com/view/does-tms-hold-promise-generalized-anxiety-disorder.

3. "Trauma," *APA Dictionary of Psychology*, accessed August 25, 2025, https://dictionary.apa.org/trauma.

Chapter 4

1. "Anxiety Disorders," National Alliance on Mental Illness, accessed August 21, 2025, https://www.nami.org/About-Mental-Illness/Mental-Health-Conditions/Anxiety-Disorders.

2. D. Weber, K. O'Brien, "Cancer and Cancer-related Fatigue and the Interrelationships with Depression, Stress, and Inflammation," *Evidence-Based Complementary Alternative Medicine* 22, no. 3 (2017).

3. C. Heim, P. M. Plotsky, C. B. Nemeroff, "Importance of Studying the Contributions of Early Adverse Experience to Neurobiological Findings in Depression," *Neuropsychopharmacology* 29, no. 4 (2004): 641–48.

4. David Chapman, *Philippians* (Christian Focus, 2012), 251.

5. Augustine, *On Christian Doctrine* (Beloved Publishing, 2014), II, 18.

6. American Psychiatric Association, *Diagnostic and Statistical Manual of Mental Disorders: DSM-5-TR*, 5th ed., text rev. (American Psychiatric Association, 2022), 250–54.

7. G. Fricchione, "Clinical Practice: Generalized Anxiety Disorder," *New England Journal of Medicine* 351, no. 7 (2004): 675–82.

8. D. S. Baldwin, I. M. Anderson, D. J. Nutt, et al., "Evidence-Based Pharmacological Treatment of Anxiety Disorders, Post-Traumatic Stress Disorder and Obsessive-Compulsive Disorder: A Revision of the 2005 Guidelines from the British Association for Psychopharmacology," *Journal of Psychopharmacology* 28, no. 5 (2014): 403–39.

9. Hettema, Neal, Kendler, "A Review and Meta-Analysis of the Genetic Epidemiology of Anxiety Disorders," 1568–1578.

10. G. A. Leskin, J. I. Sheikh, "Lifetime Trauma History and Panic Disorder: Findings from the National Comorbidity Survey," *Journal of Anxiety Disorders* 16, no. 6 (2002): 599–603.

11. C. A. Brook, L. A. Schmidt, "Social Anxiety Disorder: A Review of Environmental Risk Factors," *Neuropsychiatry Dis Treat* 4, no. 1 (2008): 123–43.

12. American Psychiatric Association, *Diagnostic and Statistical Manual of Mental Disorders: DSM-5-TR*, 215.

Chapter 5

1. B. Lee, Y. Want, S. A. Carlson, et al., "National, State-Level, and County-Level Prevalence Estimates of Adults Aged ≥18 Years Self-Reporting a Lifetime Diagnosis of Depression—United States," *Morbidity and Mortality Weekly Report* 72 (2023): 644–50.

2. P. E. Greenberg, A. A. Fournier, T. Sisitsky, C. T. Pike, R. C. Kessler, "The Economic Burden of Adults with Major Depressive Disorder in the United States (2005 and 2010)," *Journal of Clinical Psychiatry* 76, no. 2 (2015): 155–62.

3. J. D. Rosenblat, R. S. McIntyre, G. S. Alves, K. N. Fountoulakis, A. F. Carvalho, "Beyond Monoamines-Novel Targets for Treatment-Resistant Depression: A Comprehensive Review," *Curr Neuropharmacol* 13, no. 5 (2015): 636–55.

4. D. Weber, K. O'Brien, "Cancer and Cancer-Related Fatigue and the Interrelationships with Depression, Stress, and Inflammation," *Journal of Evidence-Based Complementary Alternative Medicine* 22, no. 3 (2017): 502–12.

5. C. Heim, P. M. Plotsky, and C. G. Nemeroff, "Importance of Studying the Contributions of Early Adverse Experience to Neurobiological Findings in Depression," *Neuropsychopharmacology* 29, no. 4 (2004): 641–48.

6. C. R. Pryce, J. Feldon, "Long-term Neurobehavioural Impact of the Postnatal Environment in Rats: Manipulations, Effects and Mediating Mechanism," *Neuroscience and Biobehavioral Reviews* 27, no. 1–2 (2003): 57–71.

7. American Psychiatric Association, *Diagnostic and Statistical Manual of Mental Disorders*, 5th ed., text rev. (American Psychiatric Association, 2022).

8. Richard Baxter, *Depression, Anxiety, and the Christian Life,* revised and updated by Michael S. Lundy (Crossway, 2018), 51.

9. American Psychiatric Association, *Diagnostic and Statistical Manual of Mental Disorders: DSM-5-TR*, 160.

10. American Psychiatric Association, *Practice Guideline for the Treatment of Patients with Major Depressive Disorder*, 3rd ed. (American Psychiatric Publishing, 2010). (Reaffirmed October 31, 2015.)

11. American Psychiatric Association, *Practice Guideline for the Treatment of Patients with Major Depressive Disorder*, 169.

12. American Psychiatric Association, *Diagnostic and Statistical Manual of Mental Disorders: DSM-5-TR*, 125–28.

13. Beverly Merz, "Six Common Depression Types," Harvard Health Publishing, October 13, 2020, www.health.harvard.edu/mind-and-mood/six-common-depression-types.

14. American Psychiatric Association, *Diagnostic and Statistical Manual of Mental Disorders: DSM-5-TR*, 215–21.

15. B. N. Gaynes, N. Gavin, S. Meltzer-Brody, et al., "Perinatal Depression: Prevalence, Screening Accuracy, and Screening Outcomes," *Evid Rep Technol Assess (Summ)* no. 119 (2005): 1–8.

16. O. Vesga-López, C. Blanco, K. Keyes, M. Olfson, B. F. Grant, D. S. Hasin, "Psychiatric Disorders in Pregnant and Postpartum Women in the United States," *Arch Gen Psychiatry*, 65, no. 7 (2008): 805–15.

17. M. Trangle, T. M. Gursky, R. Haight, et al., Institute for Clinical Systems Improvement, *Adult Depression in Primary Care*, 17th ed., accessed June 21, 2023, available at https://www.icsi.org/wp-content/uploads/2019/01/Depr.pdf.

18. Merz, "Six Common Depression Types."

Chapter 6

1. Richard Baxter, *Depression, Anxiety, and the Christian Life,* revised and updated by Michael S. Lundy (Crossway, 2018), 67.

2. Philippe Gauvreau and Stephane Bouchard, "Preliminary Evidence for the Efficacy of EMDR in Treating Generalized Anxiety Disorder," *Journal of EMDR Practice and Research* 2, no. 1 (March 2008): https//doi.org/10.1891/1933-3196.2.1.26.

3. Wendy Suzuki, "How to Calm Your Anxiety, from a Neuroscientist, the Way We Work," TED Series, YouTube, March 22, 2023, https://www.youtube.com/watch?v=FpiWSFcL3-c.

Chapter 7

1. Health Quality Ontario, "Repetitive Transcranial Magnetic Stimulation for Treatment-Resistant Depression," accessed June 21, 2023, https://www.hqontario.ca/Evidence-to-Improve-Care/Health-Technology-Assessment/Reviews-And-Recommendations/Repetitive-Transcranial-Magnetic-Stimulation-for-Treatment-Resistant-Depression.

2. J. S. Perrin, S. Merz, D. M. Bennett, et al., "Electroconvulsive Therapy Reduces Frontal Cortical Connectivity in Severe Depressive Disorder," *Proceedings of the National Academy of Sciences USA* 109, no. 14 (2012): 5464–68.

3. R. P. Garay, C. A. Zarate Jr., T. Charpeaud, et al., "Investigational Drugs in Recent Clinical Trials for Treatment-Resistant Depression," *Expert Rev Neurother* 17, no. 6 (2017): 593–609.

4. M. Trangle, T. Gursky, R. Haight, et al., Institute for Clinical Systems Improvement, *Adult Depression in Primary Care*, 17th ed., accessed June 21, 2023, https://www.icsi.org/wp-content/uploads/2019/01/Depr.pdf.

5. S. Akhondzadeh, H. Fallah-Pour, K. Afkham, A. H. Jamshidi, F. Khalighi-Cigaroundi, "Comparison of Crocus Sativus L. and Imipramine in the Treatment of Mild to Moderate Depression: A Pilot Double-Blind Randomized Trial," *BMC Complement Alternative Medicine* 4, no. 12 (2004).

6. R. N. Golden, B. N. Gaynes, R. D. Ekstrom, et al., "The Efficacy of Light Therapy in the Treatment of Mood Disorders: A Review and Meta-Analysis of the Evidence," *American Journal of Psychiatry* 162, no. 4 (2005): 656–62.

7. Mark Vroegop, *Dark Clouds, Deep Mercy* (Crossway, 2019), 18.

Chapter 8

1. See also the NASB 1995, NASB 1977, LSB, BLB, and Aramaic translations; see https://biblehub.com.ephesisans/1-10.html.

2. J. C. Ryle, *Holiness* (Banner of Truth, 2014), 84.

3. Ryle, *Holiness*, 170.

4. Ryle, *Holiness*, 95.

5. Eti Ben Simon, Aubrey Rossi, Allison G. Harvey, et al., "Overanxious and Underslept," *Nature Human Behavior* 4 (2020): 100–110, https://doi.org/10.1038/s41562-019-0754-8.

6. Simon, Rossi, Harvey, et al., "Overanxious and Underslept," 100–110.

7. "11 Reasons Spurgeon Was Depressed," The Spurgeon Center for Biblical Preaching at Midwestern Seminary, July 11, 2017, https://www.spurgeon.org/resource-library/blog-entries/11-reasons-spurgeon-was-depressed/#:~:text=Spurgeon%E2%80%99s%20depression%20didn%E2%80%99t%20hinder%20his%20ministry%20%E2%80%93%20-in,multi-faceted%20empathy%20for%20the%20problems%20facing%20his%20flock.

Chapter 9

1. Richard Baxter, *Depression, Anxiety, and the Christian Life,* revised and updated by Michael S. Lundy (Crossway, 2018), 160.

Chapter 10

1. N. T. Wright, *Surprised by Hope* (HarperOne, 2008), 96.

2. Westminster Confession of Faith, chapter 32, "Of the State of Men After Death, and of the Resurrection of the Dead," accessed August 8, 2025, https://thewestminsterstandard.org/the-westminster-confession/#Chapter%20XXXII.

3. Randy Alcorn, *Heaven* (Tyndale House, 2004), 106–7.

4. Alcorn, *Heaven*, 133–34.

5. J. C. Ryle, *Holiness*, published by readaclassic.com, 2010, 243.

6. Jonathan Edwards, "The True Christian's Life, a Journey Towards Heaven," in *The Works of President Edwards,* vol. 4 (Leavitt & Allen, 1852), 575.

7. Jonathan Edwards, *Charity and Its Fruits* (Trumpet Press, 2014), 198.

OTHER RECOMMENDED B&H BOOKS

AVAILABLE WHERE BOOKS ARE SOLD.

B&H PUBLISHING®